W9-AFA-585

Bruce C. Brown

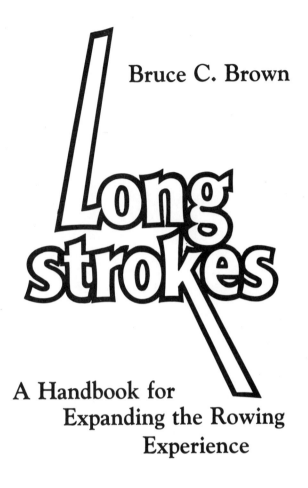

Long strokes

A Handbook for
Expanding the Rowing
Experience

International Marine Publishing Company
Camden, Maine

© 1988 by Highmark Publishing Ltd.

All rights reserved. Except for use in a review, no part of this book may be reproduced or utilized in any form or by any means, electronic or mechanical, including photocopying, recording, or by any information storage and retrieval system, without written permission from the publisher.

Published by International Marine Publishing Co., a division of Highmark Publishing Ltd., 21 Elm Street, Camden, Maine 04843.

Designed by Ken Gross.

Typeset by Camden Type 'n Graphics, Camden, Maine.

Printed and bound by Capital City Press, Montpelier, Vermont.

All photographs by the author unless otherwise noted.

Drawings on pages 4, 25, 54, 55, 104, 126, 128, by Beverly Ann Kelly.

10   9   8   7   6   5   4   3   2   1

Library of Congress Cataloging-in-Publication Data

Brown, Bruce C. (Bruce Clifford), 1945–
   Long strokes.

   Includes index.
   1. Rowing.   I. Title.
GV791.B842   1988   797.1'23   87-29891
ISBN 0-87742-950-2

For Betsy, for all the same reasons as the last time, and more.

Contents

Acknowledgments

Thanks to Karen Carlson, John Garber, Bob Jarvis, and Shirwin Smith, all fine rowers, who gave unstintingly of their time to share their thoughts, and who allowed me to quote them. Without their help this would have been a lesser book.

A special thanks to Chris Maas and Gordie Nash, not just for their help with this book, but also for their contributions to the sport of open-water rowing.

Author's Note

After much thought and debate, I've ignored the gender-neutral term *oarsperson* in favor of the more traditional *oarsman*. This is not intended as a slap in the face to feminists (of either gender) or women rowers—I'm simply more comfortable with the traditional term.

Like any sport, rowing has its own specialized vocabulary. In this work, I have chosen to use the common terms *oar* and *rowing* interchangeably with their more correct counterparts *scull* and *sculling,* and in doing so, I hope I haven't offended too many purists. As I've used the terms, a *recreational rowing boat* is any boat rowed for pleasure—from a stable, heavy dory to a swift shell. *Recreational shells* are longer and narrower than other rowing boats, yet not as long or narrow as collegiate and Olympic racing shells. They always have sliding seats and outrigged oarlocks and are usually decked over. The toughest distinction to make is that between *open-water shells* and *recreational shells,* because a fine and sometimes personal line divides the two, and sometimes a boat can be pushed across that line with the proper modifications. Open-water shells are recreational shells that can be taken offshore safely in moderate to rough (but not extreme) conditions. They must have a self-bailer and a sealed cockpit; they must be decked over; they need to be light enough for maneuverability, strong enough to withstand a punishing chop; and they should have an easy motion in rough water. The domain of this book is all recreational rowing boats, but with an emphasis on those, whether traditional peapods or modern shells, that can be used safely in open waters.

My comments on boatbuilding and design are those of an oarsman with nearly 30 years' experience, not of a qualified builder or designer, and should be taken as such. Throughout the book, some non-rowing products are mentioned by brand name because I have had personal experience with them or know people who have. The mention of a brand name should not be construed as an endorsement of either the product or the company.

Introduction

Distance or endurance rowing seems to be capturing the attention of increasing numbers of people. Recently there have been articles in several boating magazines about long-distance trips under oars. *Small Boat Journal* ran a three-part article by John Garber on his 150-mile row along the Maine coast. Concurrently, *Northwesting* published a three-part feature by Chris Cunningham on his journey down the Ohio and Mississippi rivers from Pennsylvania to Florida in a home-built rowing boat. There have also been articles on rowing from Washington State to Alaska, and the Catalina to Marina del Rey race has received national attention in several magazines. Endurance rowing has also moved into the mainstream: *Outside* featured a cover picture of Ned Gillette and the boat he plans to row to Antarctica. There have been books about transatlantic and transpacific rowing adventures. But what does all this recognition and publicity mean to the average rower in the late 1980s? The biggest advantage of this coverage might be that the rower who wants to undertake a long journey under oars is not automatically dismissed as a lunatic.

One of the pleasures of rowing is that it is an intensely personal sport. A hundred different people can row a hundred different types of boats a hundred different ways and none of them will be wrong. Not only can you row what you want the way you want to row it, but you can set your own goals. In this way,

1

endurance rowing means something different to every oarsman. To the person who uses his rowing boat for exercise and regularly rows a lap or two around his harbor, "endurance rowing" could be a 9- or 10-mile row in the open ocean. To someone who is used to rowing 9 or 10 miles on open water, an endurance row could be 15 or 20 miles to another harbor or launching area. The point is, endurance rowing is whatever each individual wants to make it.

The purpose of this book is not to encourage everyone to row across oceans, but simply to broaden his or her rowing horizons. Well-known open-water racer and boatbuilder Gordie Nash has made three attempts to row the rough 60-mile round trip from San Francisco to the Farallon Islands. He has succeeded only once and says, "You learn more from the times you don't make it." We can all set our own goals, and whether we succeed or not, in trying to attain them we will have learned and grown. This book is written to help you try.

Chapter One

Getting Started

My own first long-distance row was a comedy of errors and, if reaching one's goal is the measure of a cruise's success, a failure. I also learned more from that journey than from any other single rowing adventure in nearly 30 years of rowing. I was 17 or 18 at the time, with all the self-assurance that the age imparts. In those days, I spent long hours rowing a fiberglass Schock dory from the rocky cove beneath my grandmother's Laguna Beach home.

The dory, which lived upside down on a wooden rack built onto a rock, was a nearly perfect boat for going in and out through the surf. Fifteen and a half feet long with a 4-foot beam, she was designed along the lines of a wooden Gloucester dory from the coast of New England. At 120 pounds, she was reasonably light, and her flared sides made her very dry even while going through the waves. There was an outboard motor well aft of the single thwart, but since there was no motor, an inset was kept in the well, producing a fair bottom. I built a wooden lid for the top, making the well a secure storage area. Molded-in bow and stern compartments provided emergency flotation, and power was supplied by a pair of 7-foot spruce oars with straight blades.

My daily rowing could not be considered training—it was fun. There were short rows out to the offshore rocks, longer ones to other coves to visit friends, an occasional 16-mile round trip to Newport Harbor, and sometimes just a day spent in the boat

3

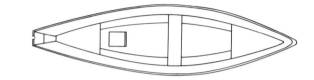

A Schock dory,
the boat the author
used for his first
long row.

rowing for the sheer pleasure of the feeling. I'd had the boat for about two years and had probably put 2,000 miles on her before my first real adventure. Between the dory and the boats I rowed before her, I had learned a lot, but I had only scratched the surface of what there was to know.

A friend of mine had rowed a similar dory just over 100 miles from Santa Barbara to Laguna Beach. This was how I first became aware of endurance rowing, and I found the thought intriguing. I decided to attempt a row from Laguna Beach to San Diego, about 60 miles down the coast. The decision to go down, rather than up, the coast was probably subconsciously based on my familiarity with the prevailing northwesterly winds. In retrospect, I doubt I gave any conscious thought to the winds; I certainly didn't give much thought to anything else about the trip. I arranged for a girlfriend to hang around near her telephone so that she could drive down and pick me up when I called, gathered a modicum of gear and provisions, and set off.

I had the good sense to leave at dawn, while the wind and sea were quiet. In the early 1960s, Oceanside was the only harbor between Laguna Beach and the twin harbors of Mission Bay and San Diego. Dana Point Harbor had yet to be constructed; the area was a rocky surfing spot known as "Killer Dana." In fact much of the coastline between Laguna Beach and San Diego was made up of surfing beaches or controlled by the inhospitable Marine Corps. Conveniently located 30 miles south of my starting point, Oceanside promised to be a perfect spot to spend the single night planned for the voyage.

I don't remember exactly what I took on that row, but I have vivid memories of many of the things I didn't take and wished I had. Provisioning consisted of going through the garage and grabbing things, then raiding my grandmother's refrigerator. My small bailer would have been totally inadequate had I really needed it, and I don't remember there being a life preserver aboard, but I do know that I had plenty of chocolate chip cookies. One's priorities change as one grows older.

I didn't make Oceanside that first day. I had brought a surfboard, strapped sideways across the stern, and stopped off Lower Churches (one of the surfing spots on the grounds of Camp Pendleton where access was denied by the Marines) to ride some waves. By the time I got back on track, I had lost several hours of rowing time. Darkness found me about 7 miles north of my day's goal. I didn't want to row into a strange harbor at night and look for a place to sleep, nor did I like the idea of landing on an unknown beach on a Marine base in the dark. There was only one other option: spend the night in the boat. This was when I first realized how pitifully ill-prepared I was.

From Churches south, I had been paralleling the outside edge of dense kelp beds. I understood that there was a very real chance of being run down in the night by a passing boat (there were no lights on the dory), so I slowly rowed deep into the kelp. The theory was that speeding powerboats would avoid the kelp and, therefore, me as well. Of course there was no anchor, so to hold my position, I tied a short bow line to a heavy stalk of kelp. As soon as I'd made the dory fast, I became aware of the pounding surf on the beach 150 yards away. I was tied to a piece of kelp by a line that would probably chafe through the seaweed. I was between an unknown beach with breaking surf and the open sea, where there was the danger of being run down by a larger vessel. I had no light, no way to heat food or water, and inadequate clothing. The only bright spot was that I was reasonably sure the sun would come up the next morning.

There was no room to stretch out in the dory, and I doubt that sleep would have come anyway. I was constantly worried that the line would cut the kelp and I would be washed ashore in the breaking surf, to be rescued by gun-toting Marines who would treat me as a trespasser. Many people think of Southern California as a land of constant warmth. I understand that a temperature of 49 or 50 degrees is not life threatening, but when it is accompanied by heavy, wet fog, and you're spending the night in a small boat, wearing still-wet swimming trunks, a T-shirt, and a light jacket, and eating a soggy sandwich and chocolate chip cookies, it is less than pleasant. It was a long night.

The sun did come up and the voyage continued. If I had been smart (but of course there was already ample proof to the contrary), I would have pulled into Oceanside and called for a pickup. I passed Oceanside while I was still feeling fresh and strong, reveling in the smooth water and morning sun. Besides, my pride was at stake: I had told people I was going all the way to San Diego. The northwesterly filled in early that day, giving me an extra push and strengthening my resolve to make the complete trip. If I had wanted to go back to Oceanside, I would have been rowing into ever-increasing seas and wind.

By the time I was 10 miles south of Oceanside, the wind waves were 3 to 4 feet and the wind was blowing 15 to 18 miles per hour. Striking the stern quarter of the dory, the wind and waves drove me off course, forcing me constantly to correct. The occasional wave also broke over the open stern, and I would have to keep the boat from broaching while I bailed with my tiny, inadequate bailer.

Nineteen miles south of Oceanside I was wet and tired, wishing I had never left Laguna Beach. Then I recognized the red tile roof of the La Jolla Beach and Tennis Club on shore. I had 11 miles to go to reach the entrance of San Diego Harbor, and another 4 or 5 to get to my pickup point. I knew the sandy beach in front of the Beach and Tennis Club and felt comfortable landing there.

With two strong pulls on my starboard oar, I gave up the journey. The beach at La Jolla is shallow and waves break well out to sea, but they are not powerful and I had rowed through them several times before. I impatiently waited through a set, then rowed hard after a smaller wave. The wave broke, sucking me along with it, and I rowed quickly through the white water, watching the next wave build behind me. It broke 20 yards behind the dory, and by the time its white water caught up with me, it had lost much of its punch, giving me a gentle push toward the beach. Once ashore, I called my friend to come collect me and slept on the warm sand until she arrived.

Every time I start on a row of any length, I think of that first long trip and all the things I didn't have, such as a spare oar, first-aid equipment, a life preserver, an adequate bailer (and a spare), a compass, lights, proper clothing, an anchor—the list seems almost endless. The lesson I learned from that trip was about the importance of preparation. Thoughtful, knowledge-able preparation can make the difference not only between comfort and misery, but also between success and failure, and, in the extreme case, life and death. Sylvia Cook, in the book *Oars Across the Pacific,* coauthored with John Fairfax, writes, "I learned that more than half the success of an operation of this nature is due to careful and extensive planning and preparation." You don't have to be rowing from San Francisco to Australia, or even from Laguna Beach to San Diego, to enjoy the rewards of preparation.

Planning and getting ready for a long-distance rowing excursion can be as exciting and rewarding as the trip itself. Success on the water depends equally on the preparation of the oarsman and of his craft. It doesn't do you any good to be in peak physical condition if your boat and provisions aren't ready, and the best-prepared boat and gear will not make up for weak arms, legs, or back. The condition of your equipment must match your physical condition, and both are gradually acquired.

I feel that one of the most important considerations for a neophyte endurance rower is to set realistic goals. If all your rowing time has been spent on a sheltered lake or within the confines of a harbor, it is probably not realistic to plan a long, open-water voyage or race as your first endurance row. There is nothing wrong with setting a long-distance passage as your ultimate objective, but it should be approached through more attainable intermediate goals.

If an oarsman wanted to get into open-water racing, a good long-term ambition would be the 32-mile ultramarathon of rowing, the Catalina to Marina del Rey race. This grueling race, described as "the hardest thing I've ever done" by Mark Steffy, who placed second in singles in 1986, should not be attempted by people who haven't trained and prepared adequately. Gordie Nash, who in 1986 made his ninth trip across the channel, agrees with first-timer Steffy, adding, "It's also the most rewarding." Even the experienced rower who has not competed in any long-distance open-water races will want to work up to the Catalina race through a series of intermediate hurdles. There have been many different approaches to the Catalina race, but those with the longest periods of training and preparation always seem to do best. A beginning racer, no matter how great his other rowing experience, would want to start with some of the shorter open-ocean races, advancing in distance as his skill increased. I call this the stepping-stone approach to distance rowing.

The same applies to cruising. A five-day cruise through the San Juan Islands of Puget Sound is a wonderful long-term goal, but not the best choice for a first attempt at long-distance rowing. A good intermediate achievement might be a day-long coastal row or an overnight excursion to a nearby bay or island. This could be followed by a longer two-night trip. Each of these interim goals would be rewarding in itself and would also serve as a stepping-stone to the long-term objective.

Whether you are training for racing or cruising, each session in the boat can be fun and educational. As you train, you will spend more time in the boat, learning more about her, the water, and yourself. If you have spent most of your rowing time in sheltered waters, you will want to start doing some of your training under more exposed conditions. Not only will your strength and endurance increase, so will your confidence as you learn to deal with a different environment.

As you train, your style of rowing may change, causing you to retune your boat in response to those changes. Correcting the height, pitch, or spread of the oarlocks or the settings of the buttons can improve any boat. If you are rowing in rough water for the first time, you will want to raise your oarlocks for added clearance. A current fad among open-water racers is to row with extreme positive pitch (that is, with the upper edge of the oar blade tilted noticeably toward the stern as the oar enters the water), the theory being that the blades lift the boat as you pull through. The placement of the buttons (the collar on the oar shaft that rests against the oarlock in use) controls the amount of power it takes to pull the oars through an arc, and as your distance increases, you might want to ease the buttons outboard 1/8 or 1/4 inch to lighten the stroke. Since rowing is such an energy-intensive sport (sliding-seat rowing saps energy faster than any other sport except cross-country skiing), you may want to think about lowering your stroke rate and concentrating on getting the most out of your boat's glide.

As your distances increase, new gear may be desirable. I have heard many people say, "I don't race, I don't need fancy equipment." I disagree. No one objects when a long-distance racer equips himself with the best gear he can afford. I feel the same holds true for the cruiser. Anyone who is contemplating long hours in his boat should equip himself with the best, most efficient gear he can buy. After all, a cruiser may be spending more time in his boat than a racer. Different sculls, different oarlocks, a compass, a watertight storage bag, or a special holder for a water bottle are all items you might want to add.

Your choice of clothing will probably change as you row longer distances; what is adequate for a short training row inside the harbor may not be appropriate for excursions into the open sea or across a lake. Layering lets you add and subtract clothes as you need them. Tights, which are quite warm and appropriate for short training rows, may be unsuitable for longer hauls. They can become uncomfortably hot and are difficult to remove in an unstable boat at sea.

As you learn, you may decide you want to modify your boat. Depending on the boat's design and your rowing grounds, a dodger, splash box, or bailer (see Chapter 3) might be appropriate. After modifying your current boat, your thoughts will inevitably turn to a new one. When that time comes, everything you learn in the stepping-stone stage will help you make the right choice. Training is a learning experience. Some of the changes you make in tuning, clothing, and gear will probably be mistakes, but you will learn from them. As you train, you will gradually evolve into a distance rower.

By using the stepping-stone approach to endurance rowing, you will slowly increase your ability while learning about your boat, the water, and yourself. This knowledge dictates what gear you take and what can be left behind. I'm a minimalist: I believe in taking only the bare necessities. I come by this attitude not from deep-seated machismo, but from simple laziness. I don't believe in giving a free ride to stuff that doesn't earn its way aboard the boat. Weight and drag are the archenemies of the rower. Every stroke you take is a battle against them, and every piece of equipment you choose to carry increases both. Because of these factors, you will want to weigh carefully the importance of every item carried. Some decisions will be dictated by the area in which you row, and others will be based on what you've learned about your own needs while training.

The challenge of endurance rowing starts with the decision to experience more from the sport. Each stroke of each training session brings you closer to your ultimate goal. Planning sessions around the fireplace in winter will kindle your enthusiasm and improve the quality of the time you spend on the water. It is my hope that your ultimate goal will become the stepping-stone to a new and greater challenge.

Chapter Two

The Boat

Virtually any rowing boat, with the exception of the true racing shell, can be used for endurance rowing. Many will require some modification to carry gear, make them safer, or both, and some will be more efficient than others, but almost any boat will do. Chris Cunningham made his trip down the Ohio and Mississippi rivers in a home-built Sneakbox, a rowing-sailing design that evolved from Barnegat Bay fowling boats of the last century. John Garber cruised the coast of Maine in *Gypsy Girl,* a plywood rowing-sailing skiff. Steve Gropp rowed around Vancouver Island in a 16-foot modified Banks dory. Art Hoban has cruised the Sea of Cortez in a 16-foot WEST system (Wood Epoxy Saturation Technique) Kite Wherry of his own design and construction.

Dale Lawrence rows the coasts of the Carolinas, following the Intracoastal Waterway in his 17-foot plank-on-frame Whitehall. Chris Maas and Greg Shell went on a three-day cruise in the Pacific Northwest aboard open-water shells, an Aero and a Vancouver 21. Gordie Nash has rowed thousands of open-water miles in a variety of traditional designs and open-water shells. I have cruised many hundreds of miles in a modified 16-foot fiberglass Appledore Pod. These boats differ substantially, but they did the job for their rowers. The design of the boat is not as important as the oarsman's desire to row. If you want to start doing longer rows and you have a boat, it will probably be adequate, at least to get you started.

11

The perfect boat, like the perfect rowing stroke, doesn't exist. No matter what boat an oarsman has, it seems he is constantly thinking about changes he would like to make or about his next boat. If you know what you want from a boat, however, you can come closer to perfection today than at any time in the past. The key to selecting the right boat or to modifying the one you have is not so much knowing everything there is to know, but truly understanding your own expectations. If your desire is to emulate John Garber and row 150 miles of the Maine coastline, your Pacific 24 advanced recreational shell will eventually have to be replaced by a more traditional design. If your goal is to win the Catalina to Marina del Rey race, your trusty old Banks dory will have to give way to an advanced open-water shell.

Rowing Boat Designs

Whether you have a boat or are looking for one, it is important to know something about the way different designs relate to one another. In *Stroke! A Guide to Recreational Rowing* (International Marine, 1986), Gordie Nash, former owner of Rowing Crafters in Sausalito, California, provided a chart comparing potential speed and stability for a great number of recreational rowing boats. He has graciously updated his analysis, and it appears here. As Gordie describes the chart, "It starts with the flat-bottomed work skiff at the upper left and the racing shell at the lower right. The Alden Ocean Shell is in the middle. All the boats to its right are faster, while all the boats to its left are slower. Stability and seaworthiness are ranked from the greatest at the top to the lowest at the bottom. All the boats below the Alden are less stable, and all those above it are more stable. In general, a faster boat is also less stable, as revealed in the downward slope of the plotted points. Experience shows us that faster boats are longer, thinner, lighter, and thus less stable and less seaworthy. There are exceptions."

Speed and stability are not the only criteria by which we measure rowing boats, but they are among the most significant.

Several other factors to consider when choosing a boat are summarized in the word "efficiency." Whether racing or cruising, you want an efficient craft, one that is light, stiff, and strong.

Weight is a relative term. A racing shell is light—30 pounds or less—but not an appropriate boat for open-water conditions. For practical purposes, weight should be evaluated only in the context of a given boat's design. The top open-water shells—the Pacific 24, Aero, and J-Shell—all weigh very close to 40 pounds, which is light compared with some other recreational singles that weigh over 80 pounds. The Pacific 30 and Dragonfly doubles weigh 80 pounds, light compared with a 120-pound double. Traditional designs, too, can be built light. Art Hoban's 16-foot Kite Wherry weighs 75 pounds, just over half what a 15½-foot Schock dory weighs.

All things being equal, a lighter boat is better than a heavier one, but strength and stiffness should not be sacrificed. If a boat is lightly built at the expense of strength, it is no bargain. Be sure your boat is more than strong enough for its intended purpose. Strength and stiffness are not, as some believe, interchangeable terms, and there are strong boats on the market that are not particularly stiff. If a boat is limber, it leeches power from your stroke by flexing and compressing rather than driving through the water, and it will not carry way as well during recovery.

Historically, endurance rowers interested in cruising have chosen boats from the upper left quadrant of the chart. Dories, Whitehalls, and peapods, traditional and transitional designs long known for their seaworthiness and carrying capacity, were the boats of the cruisers. Serious open-water racers went to the other end of the chart, selecting their boats from the advanced recreational category: the California Wherry, Maas Aero, Vancouver 21, and Pacific 24. Serious rowers of either persuasion tended to ignore the middle of the chart. The boats there were too slow for the racers and didn't offer the gear-carrying capacity the cruisers demanded. The boats in the middle were considered to be for beginners or amateurs.

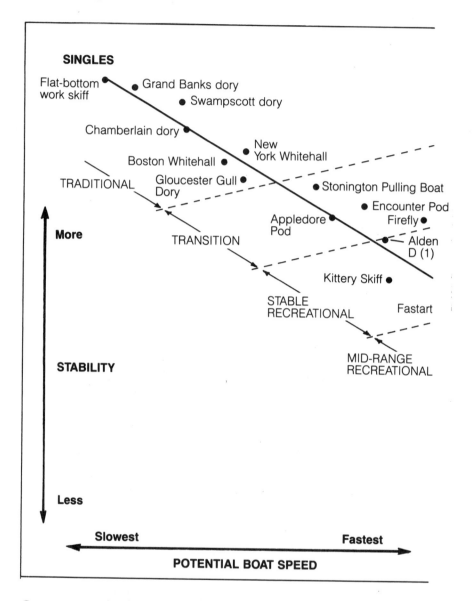

Comparative study of recreational rowing boats. Numbers in parentheses designate singles, doubles, and triples in ambiguous cases. The Monterey Bay (3) is a triple; the Alden D (1) is an Alden D rowed as a single. Note the seven regions of the chart corresponding to seven recreational rowing boat types from traditional to racing shell. Boats appropriate for open waters are not confined to any one charted region. Among the singles, for example, the Vancouver 21, Aero 21, J-Shell,

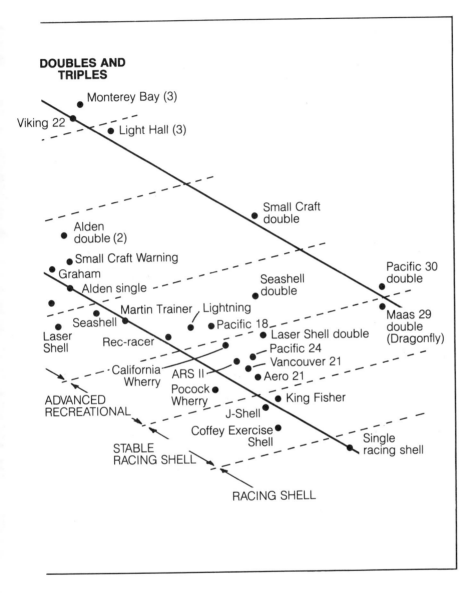

DOUBLES AND TRIPLES

Monterey Bay (3)

Viking 22

Light Hall (3)

Small Craft double

Alden double (2)

Small Craft Warning

Graham

Alden single

Seashell double

Pacific 30 double

Martin Trainer   Lightning

Seashell

Pacific 18

Maas 29 double (Dragonfly)

Laser Shell

Rec-racer

Laser Shell double

Pacific 24

California Wherry   ARS II

Vancouver 21

Aero 21

ADVANCED RECREATIONAL

Pocock Wherry

King Fisher

J-Shell

STABLE RACING SHELL

Coffey Exercise Shell

Single racing shell

RACING SHELL

Pacific 24, Pacific 18, ARS Mark II, and California Wherry are open-water boats. The Dragonfly (Maas 29) and Pacific 30 qualify among the doubles. Some other singles and doubles may perhaps serve as open-water boats, depending on the skill and size of the user, the prevailing conditions where he or she rows, and the modifications he is prepared to make to his boat. (Courtesy Gordon Nash)

Current Trends

For a long time, racing and cruising were thought to be mutually exclusive. An oarsman engaged in one or the other, and chose the "proper" boat accordingly. This no longer holds true. Some racers have become intrigued by cruising and have pressed their racing boats into service for two- or three-day voyages. Increasing numbers of dedicated cruisers have moved to faster, more modern boats.

There are several reasons for this phenomenon. First, the new boats are improving in design and construction, and many young people, who tend to be less influenced by tradition, are becoming involved in the sport. Second, relatively few of the cruising rowers can afford to take two or three weeks off for an extended trip under oars. Recreational shells lend themselves well to shorter cruises with less gear and can also cover more territory in a given time than the slower, traditional designs.

The increasing popularity of rowing boats that combine speed and reasonable stability is also attributable in part to the impact of sea kayaking on newer rowers. It seems that everywhere you look you see magazine covers, posters, or articles depicting sea kayakers cruising through some area of untouched natural beauty. They are camping on wooded beaches or skirting rugged headlands. This coverage, I believe, has influenced many recreational-shell owners to turn their boats into cruisers. The sea kayaking boom has also led to the development of gear that endurance rowers can adapt to various purposes.

Reading about some of the incredible voyages they make, someone might ask if a sea kayak were not a better choice for the person looking for a long-range endurance craft. I believe there are "paddlers" and there are "rowers," and there is seldom much crossover between the sports. "Paddlers" seem to like to face forward and take delight in the easy stroke that moves them across the water at a steady pace. "Rowers" have gotten used to facing backward, enjoy practicing the intricacies of their stroke, and revel in the glide of the boat that comes after each good pull. There are nearly as many different designs of sea kayaks as there are types of rowing boats, and knowing what you want is the key to selecting which path you want to follow.

Seen from a dedicated rower's point of view, there are advantages to each type of craft. If cash outlay is a major criterion for selection, a sea kayak is usually less expensive than a rowing boat. Smaller in volume, kayaks are normally lighter than traditional rowing boats and some low-tech open-water shells. However, a 17-foot sea kayak is usually heavier than an Aero, J-Shell, or other high-tech open-water shell. Shorter and narrower (no riggers) than open-water shells, kayaks are easier to move around. Their smaller size also allows a paddler to get into and out of tighter places than a rower can with his oars sticking out each side. Kayaks are usually more ruggedly built and easier to launch and beach, especially in rough conditions, than open-water shells. Of course, if you are rowing a well-built dory or peapod, you can launch or beach most anyplace a kayak can in similar conditions. A paddler expends less energy traveling a mile than a rower does in the same distance. While a kayak can carry more gear than a rower can easily strap on the deck of an open-water shell, it cannot carry nearly the payload of most traditionally designed rowing boats. Open-water shells, and even most traditional rowing boats, are considerably faster than kayaks, allowing the rower to cover far more distance in the same amount of time. Using the whole body, rowing is also a more complete workout than paddling. In the end, I feel that if you try both sports you will instinctively know whether you are a "paddler" or a "rower."

A Boat To Begin In

If you have decided what you want from rowing, have studied Gordie's chart, and found that your boat isn't "right" for you, you don't have to run out and buy a new one right away. No matter what boat you row, you can launch into endurance rowing the next time you go out. Simply add a little distance to your regular course. If you normally do 3 miles, do 4; if a standard row is 6 miles, go 7. Some boats are better suited to endurance rowing than others, but any boat can be rowed farther if the rower is willing to put in the effort.

Modern recreational boats are no longer the products of backyard builders. In Maas Boat Company's factory, a double takes shape alongside an Aero and a Vancouver 21, while another Aero mold waits to be filled. Note the strip of stiffness-adding carbon fiber in the unfinished Vancouver hull. Riggers are being built on the bench in the background.

Open-water boats such as the Aero, Vancouver 21, J-Shell, or Pacific 24 are perfect just as they come from the shop. They are seaworthy, unsinkable boats that can withstand any reasonable conditions. Most traditional boats—dories, peapods, and White-halls—are also naturals for endurance rowing, though some de-signs may need additional positive flotation such as foam or air bags. Rowers of recreational shells without sealed cockpits, such as the Alden, Martin Trainer, and Graham, should carry a bailer or bilge pump and probably install extra flotation before ventur-ing too far afield. This is not to imply that the flotation these boats come with is inadequate, it is just that every cubic inch taken up by foam or an air bag is a cubic inch that won't be filled up with water in the case of a swamping.

An Aero, as delivered by the factory.

Modifying a Recreational Shell

A friend of mine, Sue Greary, regularly rows a Maas Aero on extended day cruises along the Pacific coast. Since she rarely brings the boat into a beach, she laid it out to be comfortable and efficient for a long day afloat. Her equipment selections reflect a lot of thought and time, and they provide a good starting place for anyone rowing a modern recreational shell.

Sue replaced the leather clogs with track shoes (with the cleats left off) for comfort and a more secure feeling. This can be done easily by drilling out two cleat bases under the ball of the foot and matching holes in the stretcher footrest. Two small flathead bolts, dropped through from the inside of each shoe, hold them in place. When the nuts under the footrest are tightened, the

An Aero with a Strokecoach, compass, and water bottle installed and track shoes replacing the clogs.

heads of the bolts are pulled through the inner sole of the shoe to fetch up against the cleat inserts, where the rower doesn't feel them. For safety's sake, the heels should be loosely tied down, allowing just 2 or 3 inches of lift. Also in the interest of safety, the shoes should be one size larger than necessary, and they should not be laced too tightly.

She drilled a pair of holes in the upper stretcher bar and mounted a bicycle water-bottle cage behind her shoes. The cage is made of black anodized aluminum to withstand the elements; its weight can be measured in grams (the stainless steel nuts and bolts that hold it in place probably weigh more than the cage). The cage solves the problem of loose water bottles that get in the way or roll out of reach, or both, in a boat.

When she ordered the boat from Maas, she specified a bailer and compass, two important options for any endurance rower. Even though boats like the Aero, Vancouver 21, Pacific 24, and Robinson/Knect (now under production as the J-Shell) can be rowed with their small cockpits full of water, they do not perform as well. Besides, it's cold and uncomfortable. If you stop to bail with a cup in rough conditions, you often end up with more water aboard than when you started. Stopping also breaks your rhythm and can be very annoying. A loose bailer has to be stored and tied so it can't wash overboard in a swamping. The Elvstrom-style bailer, on the other hand, is mounted in the bottom of the cockpit and works on the suction principle. Open, it faces aft and sucks water out as the boat moves forward. These bailers can be open and closed as needed, or they can be left open except when launching or landing on a beach.

The compass, like the Elvstrom-style bailer, is another item borrowed from yachting. Maas removes the grip from a hand-bearing compass and mounts it on the centerline in the after end of the cockpit. There are several other good sailing compasses that can be attached to the deck abaft the cockpit, but Maas's mount is the cleanest I know.

A compass is not only a valuable safety precaution, it makes endurance rowing much easier. You can simply lay a long course for yourself and watch the compass as you row, rather than having to turn and check your direction constantly. Steering a course by compass has definite advantages over the range-astern method, in which one picks a distant object, such as a tree, rock, or building, and keeps it lined up on the stern. While this method is fine for short rows, it can become inaccurate over distance. If you are traveling several miles, you have to keep finding new landmarks. The compass provides a more accurate bearing.

Sue replaced the standard oarlocks with a pair of high-tech Stampfli oarlocks from Switzerland—expensive, but worth the extra cost. Not only can she change the pitch simply by removing a shim and replacing it with another, she can change height just as easily. This allows her to tune the boat for expected conditions each time she launches. She also has a pair of skegs, or fins: the standard Aero fin and a larger, rough-water fin that Maas offers as an option. Each day she rows, she chooses the fin to match the conditions. The rough-water fin hampers turning ability but enhances tracking in wind and waves.

The only piece of gear on her boat that is not essential to the endurance rower is a Nielsen-Kellerman Strokecoach. This electronic marvel provides a stroke-rate readout and has a time-

Mark Steffy rowing his Aero to second place in the singles class. The small splash guard, his strapped-on PFD, and stern light are all easily visible.

from-start function. It weighs less than a pound and is mounted out of the way beside the compass. Sue claims it keeps her at a good steady rate and is invaluable as a training aid.

She carries her personal gear, an extra water bottle, and snacks in a water-repellent fanny pack. While she rows, the pack rides low on her back, out of the way. When she wants something from either of the two zippered compartments, she swivels it around so that it rests on her lap.

When Mark Steffy rowed the Catalina race in 1986, he chose to set up his Aero in a very similar manner: Stampfli oarlocks, rough-water fin, bailer, bulkhead-mounted compass, shoes, and a large water jug strapped to the after side of the stretchers. Event regulations required a navigation light, a requirement he satisfied by mounting one with a suction cup aft of the cockpit. He taped over the forward part of the lens so that he wasn't staring into the light for the entire trip. He also drilled a pair of holes in the hull-to-deck-joint lip, one on either side of the boat, and ran a shock cord across the deck to strap down his life preserver. Before the race, Chris Maas built Steffy a handsome, low splash guard fixed to the hull at the forward edge of the cockpit. The result of these modifications and additions was a boat capable of making long open-water passages quickly and safely.

Oars

The battle over whether to use wooden or composite sculls still rages. Supporters of wooden sculls claim that, because of the more complex curves cut into their blades, they bite and hold the water better, are quieter in the locks, and are more aesthetically pleasing. Proponents of carbon fiber maintain that their oars are stiffer, lighter, and stronger, and require less maintenance.

The real question, as I see it, is not whether you buy wood or carbon, but whether you buy good or bad oars, and there are good and bad examples of both types on the market. If you're happy with your oars, don't change for the sake of changing. As you row longer distances, you might have opportunities to try out some of the many lengths and blade shapes available; you really should test as many as you can, to see which best suits your rowing style, before you make a change. At this writing, the vast majority of serious scullers are using Concept II composite sculls. I have a pair of beautiful wooden Pocock sculls on the wall above my couch, but I row with Concept IIs. Sue Greary uses standard Concept IIs with her cruising Aero. Mark Steffy used new, slightly longer Concept IIs in the 1986 Catalina race. Both find the sculls perfect for their uses.

Modifying a Traditional Rowing Boat

Most of the gear on these Aeros would be suitable on traditional designs with sliding seats. The only piece of equipment that would need a backup would be the bailer. If you install a suction bailer in a dory or peapod, you should be aware that it will work only while the boat is underway, and it is almost impossible to get a fully swamped dory or peapod up to speed. On any traditional design, an Elvstrom-style bailer should have either a good bucket, a bilge pump, or both, for backup. If your boat is large and stable, a good bucket is by far your best means of getting a lot of water out in a hurry. If you are in a narrower boat, you will probably find that a bailer made from a cut-down plastic bleach or water bottle works better. The cut-down bottle has a handle and can be managed easily with one hand while you hold the sculls to stabilize the boat with the other.

There is a tendency among those who row traditional designs to feel they don't need the benefits of high technology, but I firmly disagree. If you are going to spend long hours in a boat, any boat, it should be as strong, light, efficient, and comfortable as possible. Even if you don't have a sliding seat and outboard oarlocks in your boat, you can probably still make improvements in it.

Foot Braces

One very basic piece of gear many fixed-seat rowing boats don't have is a good sturdy place to brace your feet. A simple, comfortable footrest that gives good leverage will help immensely and is easy to build. You won't necessarily need to mount clogs or shoes, since your feet don't have to pull you back on your slide, but heel cups and single Velcro straps would provide a more secure footing, especially in a heavy chop or surf.

Oarlocks

You might also want to think about increasing the efficiency of your oars' arc. Racing lifeguard dories are regularly given wooden spacers between the oarlock socket and the gunwale, thereby moving the socket outboard several inches. Since each inch you move the socket outboard can increase the proper oar length by up to 3 inches, you can see that minor adjustments will mean longer oars and a longer arc. A word of caution, however: if this modification is not to become the weakest part of your boat, it must be done right. On lifeguard dories, where the gunwale is made of oak, a piece of similar wood up to 3 feet long is used to spread the load. The new oak is tapered at the ends to blend into the original gunwale, then glued and through-bolted

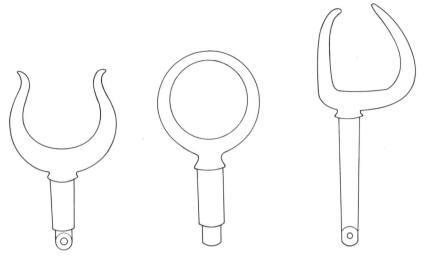

Open oarlocks   *Round oarlocks*   *Offset oarlocks*

into place. Each boat is different, but the most successful use up to eight bolts. The sockets themselves are then through-bolted to the outboard side of the new gunwale. Variations on this modification can be used on many traditional boats.

Once you've fixed the oarlock socket, what you put into it will make a big difference. Some marine hardware stores still carry pot-metal oarlocks, which should be avoided like the plague. Not only will they corrode and give your boat an unkempt look, they will also probably break, either where the shank meets the base or at the bottom of one of the horns. There are three basic shapes of oarlocks for traditional boats: the standard horns we are all familiar with; round oarlocks; and an offset design, where the forward horn is an extension of the shank. A good set of standard horns, say, Wilcox Crittenden, are wonderful for a round-shaft oar. I've never heard of one breaking, and they have no forward or aft side, so they don't have to be aligned. The only recommendation I make with these is to use the lanyard hole at the bottom of the shank to tie the locks to the boat. If you don't want to use a lanyard, put a split ring or a cotter pin through the hole.

A pair of open-horned Wilcox Crittenden oarlocks hung on a pair of dory oars. Similar locks are made by Shaw & Tenney, Perko, and Buck-Algonquin.

I don't like round oarlocks, which hold the oar captive between the button and the blade. My dislike for this type of lock probably dates back to my early days of rowing through the surf. I always used the Wilcox Crittenden locks on my boats. When I went over a particularly steep wave and dropped down its back, there was always a chance one of the oars would bounce out of its lock. With standard horns, it was an easy matter to drop it back in and pick up the stroke. I remember once using a friend's boat equipped with round locks; when the oar popped out, it took the lock with it. The lock ended up out by the blade, and while the next wave approached, I had to pull in the oar, place the shank of the lock in the socket, and start rowing again. I didn't make it and got well and properly drilled by the next wave. I know many people who don't row in surf and swear by round oarlocks. They like the fact that the lock is attached to the oar and can't be lost. True enough—but for rough-water rowing they're not suitable.

The third design, the offset, is one I've used only sparingly on traditional boats. One of its variations is standard on the Oarmaster, and I've rowed some distance with that rig. This lock comes with a vertical forward horn. If you use oars with a D-shaped loom, or shaft, these locks probably do carry more of your energy into the stroke. They are direction-specific, so they have to be set each time you put in the oars. There is at least one company making offset oarlocks for round-loomed oars. I have not rowed with these, but the concept sounds good.

Oars

Oars are one item the rower of traditional designs will want to investigate thoroughly. Changing can make a big difference, but it is expensive, so make sure before you change oars that you're happy with your oarlocks. Changing their type or moving them outboard will affect the oars you want to buy. First, the shaft shape and diameter, including the sleeves, of your oars must fit your locks. Then there is the matter of length. If your oars are too short, they will cut your arc through the water and you will lose efficiency. If they are too long, they will be out of balance and tire you unnecessarily. A good rule of thumb for determining oar length is that one-third of the oar should be inboard of the buttons. Therefore, if you know the distance from the inboard side of the lock to the centerline of the boat you can multiply that by three to get a rough oar length.

Beware: Not all oars are created equal. If the oars you are looking at have heavy blades, you will have to use shorter looms or add counterweights near the grips to balance them. You will also want to look at blade shapes. There are some short oars (under the standard 9-foot 9-inch sculling length) on the market with rudimentary cupped blades. These are definitely worth looking into, but be aware that the blades will be more fragile than standard straight blades and that the oars will be direction-specific. If you find a pair of these oars you like but are worried that the blade ends are too susceptible to damage, you can protect them with a covering. In the past, some oarsmen nailed thin copper sheaths over their blade tips. I don't recommend this, because I think nailing weakens the blade and can cause splits. Instead, I suggest glassing over the tip of the blade for added strength. This is similar to the old practice of protecting the softer wood of the blades with hardwood tips.

Traditional boat designs can accommodate more modifications than recreational designs, primarily because they are roomier. A 16-foot peapod will hold far more than a 23½-foot J-Shell. Because the traditional designs have more room, however, many rowers are tempted to keep adding gear to them, despite the fact that added weight is as great a disadvantage on these boats as it is on racing shells. Experience will dictate whether an oarsman chooses to add or remove a deck, or to install splash guards or dodgers. For instance, in Southern California, where conditions are usually mild, I have rowed thousands of miles in open traditional designs with no serious problems, though I finally added a dodger to my latest boat (see Chapter 3). The dedicated cruising rower can also consider increasing his range by adding a small sailing rig to his traditional boat (see Chapter 9).

An open-water shell, by contrast, is not nearly as versatile when it comes to modifications. You can bolt one or two items to it, change the fin, and add a splash guard, but the boat remains essentially the same as it was when it arrived from the dealer.

Buying New

If you are buying a new boat, the time you spent establishing your rowing goals and understanding your strengths and weaknesses will pay off. Never before have there been so many different designs on the market. Your chances of finding the right boat are high, but there will also be a lot of tempting boats that do not fulfill your needs. Remember that you can make short cruises in a recreational shell, but you will be hard pressed to race a traditional design successfully. If your goal involves some long races and an occasional overnight cruise, you will want to look at the advanced open-water shells. These boats are relatively easy to compare and evaluate. Gordie Nash's chart (see page 14) will give you a good place to start. Dealers and builders are usually more than happy to talk to you about their products. If, however, it is your goal to follow the oar puddles of John Garber and cruise 150 miles of the Maine coast, or to emulate Steve Gropp and circumnavigate Vancouver Island, or to go anywhere you will have to spend a night aboard, look at the traditional designs. If you buy one of these and then feel you must enter an occasional race, there is usually a class that will accommodate you.

If you do not live near an active rowing center, traditional boats may be harder to find and evaluate. There are shops that specialize in replicas of traditional designs that will be happy to help you, but you need to be well informed. There are major differences among peapods, Whitehalls, and dories, and even among boats of the same type such as Banks dories, Beachcomber dories, and St. Pierre dories.

Some boats on the market today use the names of well-known traditional designs, yet bear little or no resemblance to their namesakes. These are not necessarily bad boats, but to me the traditional name suggests certain qualities and abilities that the modern versions may not share. Fortunately, there are several good books on the subject of traditional boats (see Suggestions for Further Reading). If you are not well informed about the features that make each of these designs unique, it would be a good idea to do some reading before you go looking for a boat. I've heard many a new boat owner lament that his beautiful acquisition isn't what he expected it to be. In most cases, the owner bought his boat on the strength of another person's recommendation or for its looks. The person who recommended the boat may have had the best intentions, but what is right for one is not right for all. Do your homework. Your research will stand you in good stead while you are shopping, and knowing something about the history of the design you choose will probably make you a better oarsman.

Whether you plan to buy a recreational shell or a traditional design, there are some factors that will be more important to you as an endurance rower than to the average boat buyer. Wood or fiberglass, it goes almost without saying that sturdy construction of the boat and all its equipment will be a top priority. Not only will you want to look at hulls, decks, and their joints, you will want to carefully examine stretchers, seats or thwarts, and riggers or oarlock sockets. Look past the paint, varnish, or gelcoat. A bright-finish wooden boat or the shiny gelcoat on an open-water shell may look beautiful, but it can hide a lot. Open inspection ports; look and feel inside. Above all, ask questions.

Don't just accept a builder or dealer's word that the boat is "high-tech" or "state-of-the-art." Look for signs that the builder may have cut corners, such as aluminum pop rivets instead of stainless steel, or polished aluminum fittings rather than brass or stainless. Ask questions about resins, types of glass, foam cores, wood, glues, and fasteners. Know that S-glass is superior to E-glass, though at least five times more expensive. Some builders do incorporate S-glass in their boats to save weight without sacrificing strength. Know that there are three types of resins—epoxy; modified epoxies, which include vinylester-modified and acrylic-modified; and polyester—and know a little bit about the properties of each.

Epoxy resin is by far the best resin on the market today. It is slightly lighter than the others, and it has greater strength, tremendous bonding ability, and high impact resistance. If flexed, it will not break down over time. It is also the hardest to work with and costs about three times more than polyester. If a builder goes to the expense and trouble of using epoxy resin, his brochures will advertise that fact.

The modified epoxies fall between epoxies and polyester. They are not as strong or impact-resistant as epoxies, nor do they bond or resist breakdown as well. On the other hand, they perform all these functions better than polyester, are easier to work with than epoxy, and cost about one-third less.

Most fiberglass boats in the world today are made from polyester resins. They are the cheapest and easiest to use, as well as being compatible with polyester gelcoat. They are also the most brittle and least impact-resistant, will break down over a period of time, and offer the poorest bonding. This is not to say boats built from polyester should be avoided—there are plenty of these boats around that have survived the test of time. You should know a little about building materials and the reasons for using them.

With changes occurring constantly in the chemical industry, it is virtually impossible to provide reliable answers to questions about material compatibility. Some people feel that certain resins work better with S-glass, while others are more compatible with E-glass. Some carbon fiber has a binding strip made to break down with epoxy resins, but that doesn't mean that it will be totally useless if it is used with polyester. You can't accept blanket statements on compatibility; the information could be several years old. Properties of materials change, and builders learn different ways to work them.

Whether your boat is E-glass or S-glass, polyester or epoxy, beware of large concentrations of mat, which adds some stiffness but is heavy for the strength it imparts. If you don't understand the answers to your questions, it is your responsibility to keep asking until you do. If the dealer can't answer your questions to your satisfaction, call the builder. A long-distance telephone call is cheaper than a boat that breaks down sooner than you expect. Talking to the builder will probably be quite educational. Remember that a foam core, when used, is vital to the boat's structural integrity, and you should know about its composition. (Foam is virtually the only core material used in rowing boats.) Does it have a proven track record? If you question the way a builder is combining materials, talk to several other builders and see what they have to say. See if you can find one or two owners of boats like those you are considering. Ask them questions: Have they had problems or similar experiences with their boats? If so, was the builder or dealer helpful, or did the relationship end as soon as the money changed hands? Several books on boatbuilding are included in the Suggestions for Further Reading. Study a few of them before talking to a builder or dealer.

Safety is another factor of great importance to the endurance rower. Most modern open-water shells are very safe boats. Their small cockpits are sealed; they hold very little water and can be rowed while awash. While not bulletproof, all the top boats are strongly built. From design to design, seaworthiness and speed vary only slightly.

Not all the boats charted as "advanced recreational" fit into the category of recreational shells. There are two whose performance has placed them in the advanced category that don't fit several of the remaining criteria. One is the original Pocock Wherry. Designed and built as a training boat for racing scullers, it is an open boat that is less stable than the others in this category. A Pocock would require some extensive modification before it could be considered fit for serious offshore work. One with a light plastic deck and extra flotation did compete successfully in several open-water races in California. To meet the demand for this type of boat, Pocock now builds a decked wherry. The other boat that does not conform to the shell type is the California Wherry. More boat than shell, she is actually a modern copy of a racing boat from the early 1900s. The California Wherry is partially decked but does not have a sealed cockpit. It is an extremely seaworthy design. The addition of an Elvstrom-style bailer makes her a perfect endurance rowing boat, as long as you don't have to sleep aboard.

The cruiser who plans to sleep aboard will have to focus on the traditional designs. None of the open-water shells have enough room. Most people need a space at least 6 feet long by 3 feet wide to sleep comfortably—quite a bit of clear deck space in a rowing boat. In most boats, you will be able to get this amount of space only if you can remove the rowing station or lift out the thwart. Be sure to check on this before you buy if you think you may want to spend the night aboard.

Once you have found one or two well-built boats that seem to suit your purpose, it is time to ask more questions. Since you will be using your boat harder than the average rower, you should give some thought to maintenance. Most open-water shells on the market today, as well as the fiberglass replicas of traditional designs, are nearly maintenance-free. You will need to keep the oarlocks and stretchers clean, and, if your boat has a sliding seat, the tracks will need to be wiped down regularly. Bolts will need to be removed occasionally and packed with white grease so that they don't freeze up, but that's about it. If you've opted for wood, you have taken on a bigger responsibility. Painting and varnishing will make demands on your time.

Many people find the time they spend on upkeep to be relaxing and enjoyable, an occasion to remember past cruises and plan future journeys. To others, maintenance is drudgery. Know how you view such chores before you make your choice.

The logistics of moving a new boat around may affect the endurance rower more than the average oarsman. The person who rows his boat three or four times a week, launching off the same beach or dock, may be able to deal with a boat that would give the endurance rower headaches. If your boat is heavy and has to be moved about either on a trailer or a cart, it might be difficult to drag up on a secluded beach. You will have to think about carrying the cart, or one or two inflatable beach rollers, with you. Weight is also a factor in open-water shells, where some can weigh half again as much as others. It is one thing to struggle to get a heavy boat from your car to the water, quite another to land it on a rocky beach and get it ashore before the next wave strikes.

Finally, there is carrying capacity of the boat to consider. This is not simply the amount of room aboard, but rather the amount of weight that the boat can comfortably carry. Please note the use of the word *comfortably*. I don't believe a boat should be loaded to its maximum; there should always be a safety margin. Remember that you are part of the payload. If your boat has a suggested maximum payload of 250 pounds and you weigh 200, this severely limits what you will be carrying. There are some very good recreational shells on the market that are specifically designed for the lighter rower. If you weigh near the upper limit of your boat's rated payload, you will have to keep this in mind when you think about strapping a watertight bag full of camping gear to the deck. When you go for a test row, think about the effect the weight of extra gear will have on the boat, and leave a safe margin for error.

Once you've chosen your boat, take a long look at the list of equipment the builder offers. Many people try to save at the time of purchase only to spend more money later by adding or replacing gear. The difference in price between standard oarlocks and adjustable ones might be just $50 at the time of purchase. If, two or three months down the line, you decide to discard the original locks for adjustable ones, you could be looking at a price of well over $100. Many builders will install shoes on the stretchers for nothing if you supply the shoes, saving you the trouble. A compass or bailer installed by the builder might be a bargain compared with buying it later and installing it yourself. On the other hand, don't get talked into equipment you don't really need. Think over your purchase very carefully.

Buying Used

Buying a used boat can save you some money, but real bargains are few and far between, because good open-water boats retain a high resale value. It is easy to let an attractive price sway you, but don't—be wary. If the boat you buy is not suitable for the kind of rowing you intend to do, or if it is falling apart, it's no bargain at all.

Shopping for a used boat involves much the same drill you would use when buying new. That is, decide what you want from rowing, then which boat or boats will best suit your needs.

Builders will frequently have a good idea where you might find a boat for sale, and dealers, if they don't handle used boats themselves, may have a bulletin board listing used boats for sale by their owners. Races are another good hunting ground for used boats. When you find a boat, don't be afraid to ask questions. Why is the owner selling? Remember that buying a boat is, by nature, an adversarial situation. The seller wants to get as much for it as possible, and you want to make the best deal you can. It is not in the seller's best interest to be too frank. Granted, this is a worst-case scenario, but it is better to be prepared to deal with someone who is not wholly candid and then be pleasantly surprised than to trust every word and be disappointed later.

When you are looking at a boat, ask other rowers who own the same type if there are any inherent problems. If there are, be sure you carefully inspect them on the boat you are considering. Ask the seller if you can have the builder (if he is nearby) or a dealer take a look at the boat. In the end, *you* must make your own decision. Is the boat the one you want, or are you making a compromise because of price? Can you live with that compromise later? Is the boat in good shape for the price? There are deals to be had, but only if you do your homework.

As I said in the opening of this chapter, there is no such thing as the perfect boat. When I was 16, rowing my first Schock dory, I thought it was the best boat in the world. Then I rowed a Catalina Wherry, a canoe-sided craft with a wineglass transom, a nearly plumb bow, and a full-length keelson. Similar in overall length to the Schock dory, but with a longer waterline, the Catalina Wherry quickly demonstrated that she was a faster boat in the open water. The Wherry tracked and carried way better. Due to its tumblehome, it was also a far wetter boat. The flared sides of the dory pushed spray away and down; the wherry seemed to invite water aboard. When launching through the surf, the wherry had a disconcerting habit of wanting to push through waves rather than ride over them. This is when I learned that all boats are compromises—some do one thing better than others, but none of them can do everything. I should probably never have rowed that wherry. I might still be blissfully rowing my dory, thinking it was the best boat in the world.

Some oarsmen are happier with their boats than other oarsmen. In a few cases, this is just dumb luck: they happen onto the boat that meets their needs. In most cases, however, an owner's satisfaction with his boat has more to do with experience and careful study. Many rowers have spent a lifetime searching for the perfect boat, a nebulous concept whose contours change with time. The search for the perfect boat can be an exercise in frustration, or it can be an exciting and rewarding quest.

Chapter Three

Making Your Boat
Suit Your Purpose

In Chapter 2, we discussed what to look for in an endurance rowing boat. Some general guidelines were offered, along with a few suggestions on how to make either an existing or a new boat more comfortable and efficient for the long row. In this chapter, we are going to look at specific case studies of oarsmen who have modified or built boats with clear-cut endurance-rowing goals in mind. Each of these boats was designed or modified to meet an experienced oarsman's special needs. An examination of those needs and the modifications that satisfied them offers much that is generally applicable to endurance rowing.

In Chapter 2, we saw how an oarsman modified her Maas Aero for day-long excursions offshore by adding a bailer, a compass, a water-bottle cage, a Strokecoach, and adjustable oarlocks. We also looked at another rower who used almost exactly the same approach to get his Aero ready for the grueling Catalina to Marina del Rey race. As noted earlier, open-water shells, because of the way they are designed and built, offer fewer opportunities for modification than the traditional designs. Therefore, it is probably more important that you buy exactly what you want in an open-water shell than in a traditional design. This does not mean that an open-water shell can't be altered somewhat, only that your options will be limited. Nor does it mean you should accept a traditional design you know is wrong for you in the hope that you can tinker with it enough to make it right.

When Greg Shell and Chris Maas decided to cruise the Pacific Northwest after the Great Cross Sound Race, they took an Aero and a Vancouver 21 (basically an Aero with a splash box that adds 8 pounds). Both are fast, seaworthy open-water shells, ideal for covering a lot of ground in a limited time. Both boats were already equipped with compasses, bailers, and adjustable oarlocks, so the remaining problem was how to carry three days' provisions and camping gear on the boats. To Maas and Shell's knowledge, no one had ever cruised in an open-water shell, so they were breaking new ground.

The two men borrowed technology from the sea kayakers and used watertight kayaking bags, which they strapped to the decks fore and aft. On the Aero, this was accomplished by drilling a series of small holes through the hull-to-deck-joint lip and using shock cords to hold the bags in place. On the Vancouver, where there was no lip, they pop-riveted small pad eyes to the decks and ran the cord through them. With modern, lightweight camping gear and provisions securely stowed in watertight bags evenly distributed fore and aft, they found the boats ideal for a three-day journey into the wilds (see Chapter 10 for details on this expedition).

If your goal is to race, or if you are interested in making fast day trips in open water, you will be interested in what Gordie Nash has done with some of his boats. Nash is probably the most visible of all open-water racers, having won races and set elapsed-time records for courses on both coasts. Until the 1986 racing season, Nash rowed production boats. As he rowed and learned, he modified these boats to improve their performance and efficiency.

His enviable racing record aside, Nash is probably best known for his "instrument panel." Over the years, he has gathered together a group of instruments that surround his stretchers and monitor both the boat's and his own performance. Arrayed at Nash's feet are a digital compass, digital knotmeter, Strokecoach (with a time-from-start function), and a real-time watch. At a glance, he can read his course, speed, stroke rate, and rowing time. Along with these instruments, all Nash's boats have been equipped with suction-style bailers and arrays of water bottles.

Gordie Nash's seat in his Pacific 30. Along with a Strokecoach, which provides stroke rate, time from start, and stroke count, there is a real-time watch, a digital compass, and a digital knotmeter. Note the thick foam pad on the seat. Gordie prefers clogs to shoes for their ventilation.

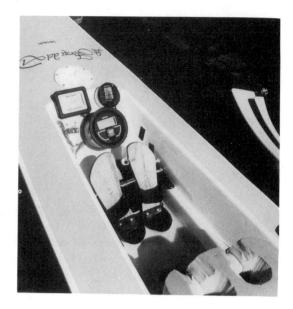

The original configuration of the Small Craft ARS (22 feet 3 inches by 24 inches by 80 pounds), a heavy but superb open-water boat. (Photo of the author by Betsy Brown)

Gordie Nash's modified ARS Mark II at the finish of the 1985 Catalina to Marina del Rey race. Note the water wings.

In 1983, Nash modified an Alden Double by stretching it to 23 feet 4 inches and set a doubles record in the Catalina race. In 1984, he dropped another Oarmaster into the same boat and gave it to the women's team of Shirwin Smith, Hillary Dembroff, and Karen "KC" Carlson for the race. In 1985, Nash rowed a 22 1/2-foot Small Craft ARS Mark II in most of California's open-water races and went East to row another Small Craft in that year's very rough Goat Island Race in Newport, Rhode Island. This boat weighed 85 pounds, was suitable for extremely rough conditions, and will be remembered for its black carbon fiber "wing." Shaped like a blunted V, the wing attached to the deck aft of the cockpit and the arms swept forward to hold the oarlocks.

By the time he was ready to do the 1985 Catalina race, Nash's ARS had undergone some interesting modifications. Small blocks of balsa were carefully shaped and bonded to both the bow and stern. They improved the hull's hydrodynamic efficiency by providing a finer entry and cleaner release. After being attached to the hull, the balsa blocks were painted over, and only careful scrutiny could detect their presence. More obvious were Nash's "water wings." Nash first used these clear sheets of 4-mil plastic in 1980 on a Martin Trainer, which he rowed to first place in his class. The plastic is duct-taped to the deck and extends to the sill of the wing, preventing water from splashing aboard.

Another boat in that year's race featured extensive Nash-inspired modifications. He turned a Small Craft Double into a triple for Shirwin Smith and Hillary Dembroff, who had rowed the year before in the stretched Alden, and their new teammate Dolly Stockman. The standard 24-foot Small Craft hull was used, but Nash built a new deck, stretching the cockpit to allow for a crew of three. The triple did well, finishing only seconds behind a larger triple rowed by three men.

In the rough 1985 Catalina to Marina del Rey race, Nash came second to Danish Olympic rower Per Hertig in another extensively modified open-water shell. Hertig rowed a boat specially put together for the race by Laser. Tad Springer, designer of the Laser shells, took one of their 24-foot double hulls, rigged it as a single, and decked it over with thin plastic sheeting to keep water out and reduce weight to a minimum. The combination of Olympic rower and long waterline proved unbeatable. The exercise demonstrated what could be done with a recreational shell when someone modifies a boat to meet a specific challenge.

If Gordie Nash hadn't already had plans for a new boat, placing second in 1985 would surely have sent him to the drawing board to design one. As it was, he had already spent several months refining the design of a double that he hoped would break the record in the 1986 race. In the past, good recreational shells with offshore capabilities had been pressed into service for

Per Hertig in the trick Laser, winning the 1985 Catalina to Marina del Rey race.

distance racing. Gordie Nash's Pacific 30 was the first open-water shell designed with long-distance racing in mind. Nash describes the Pacific 30 as a boat for the oarsman who wants to "do Catalina . . . or go out and row all day long in a high-performance, open-water racer-cruiser." He wanted a fast boat that was stable and seaworthy enough to withstand a 14- to 16-knot cross-wind.

For all Nash's experience in rowing and building boats, the Pacific 30 did not just happen overnight. After he had decided exactly what he wanted the boat to do, he had to figure out how to accomplish his goal. He spent hours rowing a Small Craft Double. Having determined that the boat had the stability he required, he factored this element into his calculations. Then he drew out the waterline, making the boat narrower as it got longer, but keeping the stability factor constant. He involved a naval architect, Bob Smith, of Mill Valley, California, in the project, supplying him with the criteria for the cockpit layout and hull shape, waterline length, stability, speed, and seaworthiness. Nash also wanted a small cockpit, so that the rowers would be as close to each other as possible to center the weight. Bob Smith drew the boat, Nash modified the design, then Smith

Gordie Nash and Kevin Strain rowing the prototype Pacific 30 to a win in the Tahoe North Shore Rowing Regatta.

revised the drawing. The plans went back and forth five times before they were finalized. After the plans were set down, and while the hull molds were being built, one final decision was made to lower the freeboard. Nash claims that this last-minute change "made the boat."

The prototype Pacific 30 had a removable stern section to make it legal for car-topping. Built from standard gelcoat and cloth, the boat weighed in at 120 pounds. It looked strong, seaworthy, and fast. The first Pacific 30 debuted at the San Diego Bay to Bay Race. A 20-mile race from Mission Bay to San Diego Harbor, the Bay to Bay Race evenly divides its distance between open and protected waters. The team of Gordie Nash and Kevin Strain won the event against some serious doubles competition, which included an old rival, Per Hertig, and his partner. Two months later, they took the boat to the thin air of Lake Tahoe, in the High Sierras, and won the North Shore Rowing Regatta. At

A close-up of the modified Latanzo rigging of the Pacific 24, the same system that is used on the Pacific 30.

Tahoe, they beat other doubles, including a racing double, on smooth water. One would have thought the boat was an unqualified success—but not Nash. He had other plans for the Pacific 30 before the Catalina race.

Nash wanted the boat lighter, so weight was shaved wherever possible. No structural compromises were made, but better, lighter materials were used. The boat's removable stern feature was eliminated, saving 15 pounds in bulkheads and fastenings. The second Pacific 30 was built of carbon fiber and was not gelcoated, though the deck was sprayed with linear polyurethane. The weight of the second boat, rigged with customized Latanzo outriggers and with all electronics installed, was under 85 pounds. The prototype Pacific 30 and the boat Nash and Strain rowed in the 1986 Catalina race were similar in that, in Nash's words, "They displaced water, two people sat in them, and they had four oars." See Chapter 11 for more on how this boat performed in the race.

A Pacific 24 (24 feet by 24 inches by 47 pounds), designed to excel in rough conditions.

Some readers may find the Pacific 30's design and modifications an extreme case. After all, not many rowers have the time, money, knowledge, or ability to design and build a race-winning rowing boat. On the other hand, a lot of technology trickles down from a project such as this. Nash took the dimensions from the Pacific 30, reduced them, and produced the Pacific 24, a single version of the boat. His building techniques will surely be adapted by others to produce lighter, stronger boats. While few rowers may ever race Pacific 30s from Catalina to Marina del Rey, many will eventually benefit from the fact that Nash built the boat.

Earlier I mentioned that traditional designs offer more opportunities for modifications. My own Appledore Pod is a good example. Four years ago, I wanted a cruising boat but discovered there was nothing on the market that met my requirements. I had

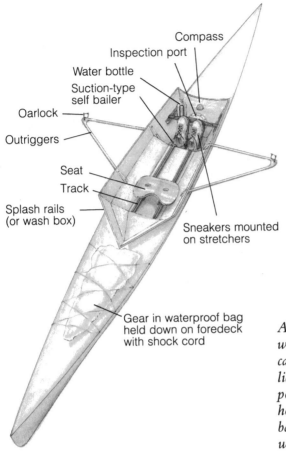

Compass
Inspection port
Water bottle
Suction-type
self bailer
Oarlock
Outriggers
Seat
Track
Splash rails
(or wash box)
Sneakers mounted
on stretchers
Gear in waterproof bag
held down on foredeck
with shock cord

An open-water shell with custom modifications. The screw-in lid of the inspection port can be used to hold captive a plastic bag containing keys, wallet, and other valuables. (Kathy Bray drawing)

owned quite a few boats by then and had some definite ideas about what I wanted and did not want in a cruising boat. I wanted a relatively fast fiberglass boat capable of doing serious offshore work. The boat had to be able to carry enough gear for a week, allow me to sleep aboard, and, if possible, accept a sailing rig. For the speed I wanted, the boat would have to be equipped with a sliding seat and riggers. For serious offshore rowing, she would have to be strongly built and seaworthy. Only a traditional design would have enough room to let me sleep aboard.

The boat that came closest to what I was looking for was Martin Marine's Appledore Pod, but there were problems with this boat. I wasn't happy with the twin boxlike stringers that ran the length of the hull, making all the deck space unusable. After rowing many hundreds of miles with an Oarmaster, I knew I wanted a rowing rig that was lighter and more efficient. Furthermore, Martin's bipod sailing rig was not what I wanted. The 16-foot fiberglass hull, a faithful reproduction of a traditional New England design, was ideal for my needs. All that had to be done was to change the interior.

We spent some time with the bare hull and came up with a few relatively simple modifications that would make her fit my requirements. The first priority was to build a good rowing cruiser, so the sailing rig was left to be fitted around the completed rowing rig. Since one of the major advantages of the Oarmaster is that it does not distribute the strains of rowing to the hull, and the Appledore was designed to be used with the Oarmaster, the hull had to be strengthened. We glassed and bolted a pair of plywood ribs to the hull near the rowing station. Flotation chambers, slightly larger than those in the stock boat, were glassed in fore and aft. The two foam-filled stringers running the length of the hull became the foundation for a 3/8-inch teak marine plywood deck. A 9 1/4-inch-square hole was cut into the deck aft of the ribs so that the stretchers of a lightweight rowing station could be dropped in. The rowing station, a skeletal wooden framework supporting a Latanzo seat and tracks and stretchers consisting of plastic heel cups and Velcro straps, was anchored in place by captive dowels, which slipped into holes drilled in the deck. The rowing station could be lifted out, and a hatch could be placed in the stretcher hole to provide a clear deck for sleeping or sailing.

The removable, hard, anodized aluminum riggers are L-shaped. The foot of each L slips into an aluminum bracket through-bolted to the hull forward of the ribs. A pair of 1/4-inch stainless steel bolts anchor each rigger in place. The pin-to-pin dimension on the finished boat is 62 inches. With my feet down against the bottom of the hull and my seat just 4 1/2 inches above the deck, *Kavienga*'s center of gravity is far lower than it would

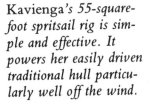

Kavienga's 55-square-foot spritsail rig is simple and effective. It powers her easily driven traditional hull particularly well off the wind.

have been with the Oarmaster-equipped boat. The weight of the deck, riggers, and rowing unit is less than that of the discarded Oarmaster. The oarlocks are Latanzo gated locks, and the original oars were 9-foot 9-inch wooden Piantedosi sculls. I cracked the back of a Piantedosi when I hit a buoy on the recovery and quickly replaced the wooden oars with lighter, stiffer Concept II composite sculls. The first addition I made to the finished *Kavienga* was to bolt a compass to the rear of the stretcher board.

Once I was satisfied that *Kavienga* would perform well as a rowing cruiser, we turned our attention to the sailing rig. I had no desire to beat into the teeth of a raging gale; I simply wanted to be able to hoist an easily stored sail and reach or run when the wind permitted. While I was prepared to be flexible on the type of rig, I did have one rigid requirement: The integrity of the hull could not be violated with any sort of daggerboard or centerboard. A boomless, unstayed spritsail rig was a perfect solution to the problem. The mast and sprit are both under 10 feet long, light and easy to store. The sail design keeps the center of effort low and puts quite a bit of canvas (55 square feet) in the air. A mahogany mast partner was located 55 inches aft of the bow and added great stiffness to the hull. The underwater foils, comprising the leeboard and rudder, are borrowed from a Naples Sabot. The leeboard attaches to a standard fitting forward, and the rudder hangs in gudgeons off the stern. (For more on sailing rigs for rowing boats, see Chapter 9.) *Kavienga* worked well and carried me many miles, but there were things that needed changing.

Occasionally I daysailed *Kavienga*—and she sailed well—but on rowing trips I would find myself lugging the sailing rig around and never using it. The rig lay in the boat, taking up space and adding weight, and it always seemed too much of an effort to rig. I love rowing downwind, and the thought of stopping, pulling in the riggers, removing the rowing station, stepping the mast, unfurling the sail, rigging the sprit, and rigging the leeboard and rudder did not appeal to me. First I stopped carrying the leeboard and rudder and now and then sailed dead downwind, steering with the sheet. These occasions were infrequent, so I just stopped taking the sail with me.

The biggest problem I had with *Kavienga* was with the raised deck. The plywood deck allowed water to collect underneath and made it hard to get at. If I took my feet out of the stretchers and slid all the way aft on the tracks, I could use a small scoop to lift water out of the hole in the deck. This was uncomfortable and inefficient. For some time, I used a hand-held bilge pump. I put the pickup in the hole in the deck, draped the flexible hose over the side, and pumped. This was far more efficient than the scoop, but meant I had to stop rowing, find the pump, and set it up. I wanted something faster and easier.

My first plan was to remove the deck, fill the area under it with blown foam, hog out a place for my stretchers, and then glass over the foam. Finally, I would mount a suction-style bailer in the foot well. The foam would give added flotation, and the bailer would be in the lowest part of the boat where the water collects. Any water the bailer couldn't handle would be where I could get at it with a scoop or a bucket. There were some problems with this solution: It would mean that in rough conditions the deck would be constantly awash. Any gear on the deck would get wet, and I, sitting just 4^1/$_2$ inches above the deck, would be sloshing through a lot of water while I rowed.

I finally decided to leave the wooden deck alone and permanently mount a bilge pump where I could reach it comfortably with one hand while still holding the sculls with the other. I mounted a small Munster Simms pump by through-bolting it to the deck just forward and slightly to port of the rowing rig. A hole was drilled in the center of the deck, and the pickup hose was brought through the deck to rest in the center of the boat. The exhaust hose was led to a through-hull fitting high on the port side. The leads may not be as fair as the manufacturer would like, but the little unit pumps a lot of water very quickly.

The other problem the raised deck gave me was that anything loose in the boat promptly rolled under it and remained inaccessible until the next time I brought the boat to a beach. I solved this problem in two ways. First, I through-bolted some guides on the top of both flotation compartments and ran shock cord through them so that I could lace gear down. I reserve this area for light gear to keep the weight out of the ends. Then I bought a pair of 6-foot-long nylon-mesh hammocks, the type used in cruising yachts to store gear and provisions. I strung one on either side, from the forward flotation compartment aft to the riggers. These hold a tremendous amount of gear and keep it handy. Everything else gets pushed into a pair of waterproof canoe bags, which are too big to slip under the deck and can be shifted about the boat to counterbalance the weight of water jugs, anchor, and the like.

The final major modification of *Kavienga*, at least to date, has been the addition of a dodger. Under certain conditions, *Kavienga* catches a lot of spray, and a dodger seemed a good solution to the problem. Since I sit low in the boat, the major consideration for the dodger was that it not block my view forward. As any oarsman knows, it's hard enough to see where you're going by twisting and looking over your shoulder, and you don't need a piece of blue canvas blocking your vision. After a little experimenting the optimum height was found. A higher dodger might keep the boat dryer, but would limit my vision too much.

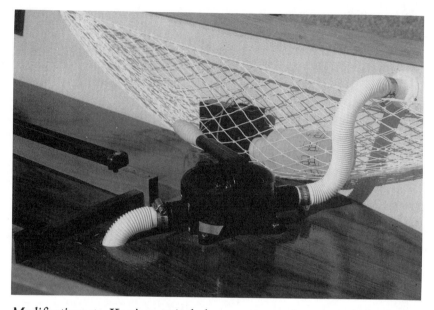

Modifications to Kavienga include a permanently mounted diaphragm pump at the forward end of the tracks and gear-carrying hammocks strung from the inboard end of the riggers to the mast partner. The hammock contains a hand-bearing compass and a water bottle.

The dodger forced me to adjust the way I raise the anchor. The anchor line is attached to a bow eye through-bolted to the hull. With the dodger in place, I couldn't reach the anchor line. The problem was solved by tying one end of a messenger line to the mast partner and looping the other around the anchor line. Now, to retrieve the anchor, I first pull in the messenger line, then grab the anchor line, and hoist.

Kavienga suits my needs better than anything on the market. The modifications I've made since her purchase have made her a far easier boat to live with. Don't be afraid to make changes in your boat. Sometimes a very minor change can make her far more comfortable or efficient. For instance, adding the permanently mounted bilge pump took less than two hours and called for nothing more complicated than a power drill, a knife, and a

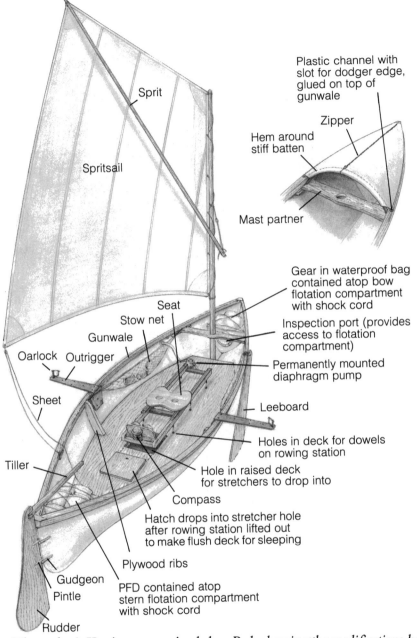

Plastic channel with slot for dodger edge, glued on top of gunwale

Zipper

Hem around stiff batten

Sprit

Spritsail

Mast partner

Seat

Stow net

Gunwale

Oarlock   Outrigger

Sheet

Tiller

Gear in waterproof bag contained atop bow flotation compartment with shock cord

Inspection port (provides access to flotation compartment)

Permanently mounted diaphragm pump

Leeboard

Holes in deck for dowels on rowing station

Hole in raised deck for stretchers to drop into

Compass

Hatch drops into stretcher hole after rowing station lifted out to make flush deck for sleeping

Plywood ribs

Gudgeon

Pintle

PFD contained atop stern flotation compartment with shock cord

Rudder

The author's Kavienga, *an Appledore Pod, showing the modifications he made for cruising. (Kathy Bray drawing)*

Warren Hansen rows Kavienga *before the dodger was added. The locations of the pump, hammocks, and stern shock cord are all plainly visible, as is the stretcher-mounted compass.*

screwdriver. I had spent more than 10 times that amount of time cursing and attempting to bail, or wrestling with the hand-held pump, before I got around to making the installation. Not only is the boat safer, more comfortable, and more efficient, I have the satisfaction of knowing that I made her that way.

Rowers do not just build custom racers, they also build custom cruisers. John Garber made his trip along the Maine coast aboard the Phil Bolger–designed, H.H. "Dynamite" Payson–built, 15-foot plywood skiff *Gypsy Girl*. John made modifications to her even during his long row. He pulled into Camden, Maine, and laid over for several days while canvas spray shields were built for the bow and stern of the boat. According to Garber, "They didn't do much but give me a feeling of safety."

He started planning a new boat at about the same time the spray shields were being built. The Maine trip followed an inside course, but Garber "began thinking about a boat that I'd be willing to take outside. I realized I would want a partially decked boat, more seaworthy and better upwind than *Gypsy Girl*. *Gypsy Girl* is basically a skiff. I rowed her upwind once or twice against

Pogy, *a unique custom-designed cruising boat. (Photo courtesy John M. Garber)*

a heavy chop; she just pounded away and didn't make much progress. This is nothing against the boat; she wasn't designed for that kind of a trip." For the new boat, Garber's main design criteria were the same as for *Gypsy Girl:* he wanted a boat that could be rowed downwind. He discarded the idea of a dual-purpose sailing-rowing craft and focused on a boat purely for rowing. He built four half-models and consulted twice with Phil Bolger and three times with Ken Basset during the process. Finally Garber made his "first attempt at drawing lines, which I loved. There are really three designs for *Pogy:* the half-model, the lines drawing, and as built. I relied entirely on Ken for construction details. She's built of plywood, and Ken's a wizard with plywood. As built, the boat has camber below the chine forward of amidships and a slight hollow aft. She is 3 feet longer than *Gypsy Girl,* partially decked, with a V-bottom. She goes to weather. My son and I rowed her to weather in heavy chop and

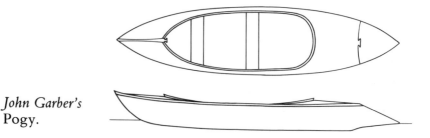

John Garber's
Pogy.

25 to 30 knots, and she only came out of the water once, and she came down soft."

Garber worked with Ken Basset for the last week of *Pogy*'s construction, and he says they were in such a rush to finish that they never took the time to weigh the completed boat, but he guesses she weighs about 200 pounds. With a single oarsman, she balances well. The load can be shifted to make her balance equally well with an oarsman on each thwart. A pair of removable planks run from side to side to brace both oarsmen's feet. There are no foot straps, heel cups, or shoes, which allows them to change their position as they row. According to Garber, *Pogy*'s hull, below the chine, has "a codfish head and a mackerel tail, full forward and fine aft. She tracks perfectly; of course, the trade-off is that she's slow to turn. It makes her hard to bring alongside a float, but, then, she was designed as a cruising boat." In other words, she was built for the long row, not to trundle back and forth across a harbor.

The first aspect of *Pogy* most people comment on is her handsome reverse transom. The idea for the stern, which evokes thoughts of some IOR racers, was to provide a long waterline and reduce weight. Garber's best estimate is that reversing the transom saved 20 pounds, or 10 percent of the boat's weight, and he hopes it gives him a little windage going downwind. During the design period, the transom received mixed reviews. Garber reports, "Ken Basset was really against that stern and gave me a couple of long-distance phone calls about it. He thought the pointed tip of the stern would drag. With beginner's luck, the boat floated with that tip about an inch out of the water. He, and other people, felt seas would run up the stern into the boat.

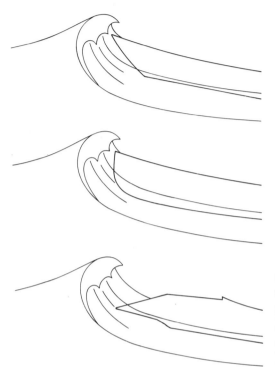

This drawing shows the sterns of three types of rowing boats being overtaken by a breaking swell. From the top they are a dory, a peapod, and Pogy.

Bolger liked it. I had less rake in the early designs, and he told me to increase the rake and it would look better. I did, and it did."

In the drawing, you can see the unique stern cleat over the transom. Garber designed it to show off the fact that *Pogy* was built out of plywood, rather than conceal it, as many try to do. According to Garber, "The boat turned out to look like a fish. We put in the caudal sensors with copper nails and the eye with a punch, and that's how she came to be called *Pogy*."

Pogy rows beautifully. For all those who expected seas to wash over the reverse transom and into the boat, Garber says, "I've been out in pretty heavy chop, going downwind, and haven't had any problems." *Pogy* already has a lot of miles under her hull, and Garber is currently planning cruises along the east coast of Texas, from Brownsville to Galveston; in the Sea of Cortez; along the Loire; and along the west coast of Ireland. *Pogy* is an example of what a dedicated endurance rower can do when he turns his mind to producing the ideal boat for his purposes.

The ultimate examples of boats designed and built for endurance rowing are not Gordie Nash's Pacific 30 or John Garber's *Pogy*; they are *Britannia II* and the boats she has inspired. Uffa Fox designed the 35-foot, self-righting *Britannia II* for John Fairfax and Sylvia Cook to row across the Pacific. She was later used by Derek King and Peter Bird to row across the Atlantic. Books have been written about both expeditions, and they are included in Suggestions for Further Reading. Currently, Ned Gillette is preparing *Sea Tomato*, an aluminum 28-footer, for the row from Cape Horn to Antarctica, and Gordie Nash is building a 34-foot single for a customer who plans to row the Pacific. In time, the design solutions required for these will affect the average endurance rower. We might not be rowing massive self-righting boats built to cross oceans, but the new breed of boats will inspire us to take on new challenges.

Chapter Four

The Oarsman

Just as modifying your boat to meet the demands of endurance rowing will make for a more successful race or cruise, so will proper physical training increase your satisfaction in your expedition. Unfortunately, the rower's condition often slips to the bottom of the list when a trip is being planned. There are so many other things to do. Few of us can simply pack up and take a week off to go rowing without making a considerable number of arrangements. There are jobs, families, and other responsibilities to consider. Planning alone can take up all our time; there seems to be none left for training.

The best antidote to these pressures is good organization, but sometimes the logistics of a rowing trip defy even the best organizers. Everything you need for your trip seems to be located in stores that take hours to reach. Important gear or provisions get left off your lists and require hurried trips to be purchased, detracting more time from your training schedule.

Working Out

Before you go for a long row, you *must* condition yourself. You must allocate the time to prepare for your row. Obviously, the best way to get ready for a rowing excursion is to row. Rowing

57

will not only prepare you physically, it will prepare you mentally as well. When you row, you remove yourself from day-to-day pressures and find the freedom to contemplate your trip.

Rowing will also teach you to pace yourself. Especially if you are rowing a sliding-seat boat, it is easy to burn yourself out after a couple of hours at the oars. You will have to develop a rowing technique that allows the boat to work to its best advantage. A slow, efficient stroke will move you along at a good rate, but not burn too many calories too fast. Since each combination of boat and person is different, rowing is the only way to learn this stroke and has the added benefit of keeping you in touch with your boat. It will be easier for you to plan what gear and provisions you need for your trip if you are in the boat on a regular basis.

Any time you spend in the boat will be time well spent, but a planned or organized rowing workout will better utilize your time. To prepare yourself for endurance rowing, you don't have to row structured-stroke or time pyramids, do interval training, or keep track of heart rate, although none of these would hurt. You will have to keep track of what you are doing and how you are doing it. Whether you're racing or cruising, endurance is your first priority. Racing strength and speed will come later. You have to be able to complete the course before you work on speed. There's an old saying in motor racing that applies to the endurance-rowing racer: "First you must finish, before you can finish first." It won't matter that you're 5 minutes ahead of the fleet on the first leg if you fade on the next. Knowing your own limits and strengths will stand you in good stead.

No matter what kind of workout you plan to do on the water, start with some stretches, especially the two described later in this chapter. Once you're in the boat, warm up; don't start pulling hard until your body is ready. Whether you're rowing sliding-seat or fixed-thwart, row for 10 to 15 minutes at quarter- or half-pressure. If you are rowing sliding-seat and want to work on your technique while you're warming up, you can start with drills such as no-feather or no-leg rowing, but don't consider either your full warm-up. After a drill, continue for a few minutes at partial pressure before getting into the workout itself.

Once you're underway, you can follow any number of paths. Most rowers find they can't do exactly the same workout each day or they get bored. If you can put four days a week into your rowing, a great training regimen is to do one long, say, 12- to 15-mile row a week and three shorter ones. The long row works on your endurance and breaks up the routine of the shorter ones. If you can row different courses for your short rows, so much the better.

Many long-distance rowers train by balancing their speed against endurance for an hour at a time. They go out and row for an hour, making note of the distance covered. The next time out, they try to go farther in the same hour. Wind, tide, and waves will obviously affect this kind of training, but it is definitely one of the best for anyone contemplating long rowing adventures.

When planning and doing your workouts, you must consider the weather and water conditions you expect to encounter on your endurance row. The closer you can come to matching these during your workout, the better prepared you will be when it comes time to race or cruise. You may not be able to match conditions exactly, but if, for instance, your race or cruise takes you through exceptionally rough water, you should not train in a protected harbor or avoid going out when it's rough. Find some rough water and get out in it. Even if you don't expect to encounter adverse winds or steep chop, it makes sense to know how to handle them. Always be prepared for the worst conditions; they will eventually find you.

If you've never experienced rowing in extremely rough conditions or through surf, get some help or advice before you go out, and don't go out alone. Find someone you respect who really knows how to row in rough water, ask for some pointers, then see if he or she will go out with you the first time or two. Just having an experienced rower there will help your confidence.

Take rough conditions a step at a time, starting with a boat that is designed and built for these conditions. Simply rowing a dory or J-Shell that can handle 15 knots of wind and the accompanying seas doesn't mean you should venture offshore in conditions you don't have the skills to handle. Ideally you will learn rough water rowing using the same stepping-stone method that you use to advance in endurance rowing. If you have rowed only on rivers or protected bays, start open-water rowing gradually, say in just five to ten knots of wind, and move up only when you are comfortable.

In a fixed-thwart traditional design, make sure your bailers (it is a good idea to carry a spare) and personal flotation device (PFD) are tied in and that anything else that could come loose is well secured. If you are rowing an open-water shell, some minor adjustments are necessary. Assuming your oarlocks have a height adjustment, it is a good idea to raise them to keep you from banging your thighs when you lift your blades clear of the chop on the recovery. Make sure your suction bailer is functioning, or that you have a manual bailer tied into the cockpit, or both. If your boat will accept a larger fin, installing one helps the boat track in rough conditions.

When you start to row in windy, choppy conditions, whether you're rowing an open-water shell or a traditional design, you will feel less stable than you are used to, and you may have trouble with your recovery. To increase your feeling of stability, shorten your arc by reducing your layback and the stretch at the catch, the two positions when you are most unstable. The problem with the recovery will be hitting the blades on the chop, but this is why you raised the locks—to allow yourself to push down hard on the handles without smacking your thighs. In extreme conditions it will be nearly impossible to avoid hitting the chop, so don't roll your oars into the full feather position. In other words, instead of rolling them 90 degrees, roll them 45. This will present the curved backs of the blades to the chop so they will strike at an angle. The impact will rock the boat, but the blade will tend to lift, minimizing the effect. You will instinctively want to hold the grips tighter, but try to avoid holding them too tightly, as it will fatigue your hands and cause hand and forearm cramping.

If you are rowing into the wind you will want to delay the rollup—the squaring of the blades before the catch—until the last possible second. This prevents the wind from hitting the backs of the blades. Even more important, it minimizes the time the squared-up blade is vulnerable to being hit by chop.

When rowing with a following wind and sea, you may find it difficult to balance the boat. Shortening your arc will help, but keep as long a stroke as possible to take advantage of the increased speed. As the waves get larger and you find yourself actually surfing, you must shorten the release considerably to keep your weight out of the bow and help prevent the nose from pearling (submarining). If the nose does start to go under, get your weight far aft as fast as you can. A diving bow can lift the stern out of the water, causing the boat to spin out, and in extreme situations this could pitch you out of the boat. If you're fast, dragging an oar blade can straighten out a spin.

None of this is intended to frighten anyone. Many open-water rowers enjoy going offshore and bashing around when it's rough, but the sea is a foreign element, and you must learn the skills needed to deal with it before you can go out and play. Just as you would not buy your first surfboard and think you could handle Banzi Pipeline, you shouldn't row an entry-level shell in 25 knots of wind.

Rowing Schools

There are several rowing schools around the country, but at this time few address the special needs of the endurance rower. Most are interested in teaching beginners to row and perfecting the strokes of flat-water scullers. There are three I know of that will take you past the beginner level in open water. Open Water Rowing in Sausalito, California, is one. They train on San Francisco Bay and offer occasional rough-water seminars. Santa Cruz Rowing School, which specializes in ocean rowing, is another. The third is the Rowing Shop in Portland, Oregon, on the Wilamette River. There may be others, so ask around.

If you find a rowing school in your area, or if you plan to travel to attend one, there are some features to look into before you put your money down. Remember that even though they are teaching and you are learning, you are the customer and they are providing a service for which you are paying. It is your right to look the school over, meet with the coaches, and ask as many questions as you want.

First check out the equipment. You can tell a lot about a school by the selection and condition of the equipment it offers. If the boats and oars are old-fashioned and poorly maintained, look around for another school. Find out if they teach what you're interested in. If the chief instructor is a national or Olympic champion intent on training other flat-water racers, look elsewhere. Then look for a low student-to-teacher ratio. By the time you have reached the intermediate level, you will need to have individual attention. Look for coaches who teach from shells, rather than from shore or a launch, so that you can watch them row. If your school offers videotaping, so much the better. If you can find a good school, a few hours spent training there will be worth far more than the same amount of time training on your own.

Getting in Shape

The success of your long passage or cruise will depend greatly on your preparation and physical condition. If you can only make the time to get into the boat once or twice a week, or if you live in a climate where you can't row year-round, you still have to do something to get or stay in shape. In the late 1980s, it seems there is a gym or fitness club on nearly every corner, offering stationary cycles, weights, jogging tracks, swimming pools, and a variety of exercise machines. As an oarsman you know the need for flexibility; strong back, legs, and arms; and a powerful cardiovascular system. If you go to a club and explain to an instructor why you're there, he or she will probably be able to design a workout for your needs. If not, change instructors or clubs.

If you don't have a club near you, or if you don't like the idea of working out surrounded by mirrors and people in designer tights, you can devise your own exercise regimen. Any stretching you do will help your rowing, but the most valuable stretches are those used by runners and gymnasts. Whatever other stretches you do, there are two you should include in your exercise program and practice each time before you row. The first will stretch your hamstrings, which are vital to getting the proper forward lean at the recovery. Stand with your feet together and bend at the waist, letting your arms drop and keeping your legs straight. Don't "bounce" to get your hands closer to the floor, just hang. The longer you hold this stretch, the better, but don't force it. The second stretch will work your back, which is important both to your lean-forward at the catch and to your layback at the release. Lie on your back and swing your legs over your head so that your knees flank your head, as close to the floor as you can get without strain. You may have to support your hips with your hands when you first do this exercise. As with the first stretch, don't force things, just let your body stretch into the position.

There are other sports complementary to sculling that will increase your stamina and strength and can be added to your exercise program as your lifestyle permits. As long as your shins and knees can take it and you don't get bored, running can be beneficial. As an aerobic exercise, running will build up your capacity for long-distance rowing. Jumping rope also falls into this category. Cycling is another good sport for the cardiovascular system and the legs, but, as with running and jumping rope, you will need to complement it with exercises for your upper body. A stationary cycle, especially one of the new ones with electronic readouts to monitor your progress, is good. In some climates, this may be the only option, but, in my opinion, a real bike is better. A real bike gets you outside and works on your balance and timing. If you don't have the time for a long daily run and would rather spend money on a new set of sculls than on a bicycle, you can always run stairs. Running stairs is a great workout, takes practically no time, and can be done almost anywhere. A few minutes spent running on stairs provides the same benefit for your legs and cardiovascular system as a much longer time spent running on the flat.

The 22-Minute Drill

If you don't want to or can't run, jump rope, or cycle, there is something else you can do—the 22-Minute Drill. Presented in *Stroke!* (International Marine, 1986) as a way for beginning or intermediate scullers to get or stay in shape, it is also a valuable tool for the experienced racer or cruiser. This drill can be done at home with minimal equipment (a bar and some weights) or at a health club with free weights. As the name implies, it is not a time-consuming workout, so it fits easily into anyone's schedule. The drill works your respiratory system and increases your overall strength. The use of free weights, as opposed to weight-lifting machines, has the added advantage of improving coordination, balance, and timing. Free weights also work opposing muscle groups, keeping them strong to prevent injury.

The 22-Minute Drill consists of seven exercises. After working your way up to the full drill, each exercise is repeated 10 times per cycle, and the entire cycle is repeated 6 times, all within 22 minutes. In order, the exercises are: power clean, bent-over rows, snatch, squats, dead lifts, military press, and curls. When you start, you will want to be conservative about the weight you load on the bar. The drill will make you sore even though it doesn't feel that way at first, so start light. A man of average size should start at 40 pounds, but if you have no weight-lifting experience or feel that 40 pounds is too heavy, go down to 30. In the beginning, the amount of weight on the bar isn't important, it's completing the drill that counts. It would be better for you to do the drill with 20 pounds of weight on the bar than to quit after 10 minutes with 40 pounds. In the beginning, repeat the cycle only 3 times, because, as with sculling, the full 22-Minute Drill is something you will have to work up to. No matter how long you've been on the program, do the 22-Minute Drill only 3 times a week.

After you do some stretches to limber up, check the clock and start the drill with the power clean. Start with the bar at your ankles, not touching the ground, knees bent, buttocks tucked under, and head up. Push up with your legs, then with your back, and your arms will carry the bar to your chin. Then slowly lower the bar back to your ankles. This exercise is directly related to rowing and works your legs, back, and arms.

After 10 repetitions of the power clean, move to bent-over rows. With your legs straight but not locked, lean over so that the bar hangs toward the ground from straight arms. Keeping your legs and back straight, lift the bar 10 times. Bent-over rows work your lats (latissimus dorsi) and your lower back.

The third exercise, the snatch, starts with the bar on the ground. This is the only time the bar should touch the ground during a cycle. You will bend your legs, pick up the bar, then thrust with your legs and straighten your back; your arms will finally put the bar over your head. Along with working your legs, back, and arms, the snatch will improve your coordination and balance more than any other exercise in the drill.

After 10 repetitions of the snatch, move to the squats. Place the bar behind your head, resting it on your shoulders. With your back straight and head up, bend your knees to about, but not past, 90 degrees, then straighten your legs. Squats are like doing deep-knee bends, but with weights on your shoulders. The squats exercise the quadriceps, hamstrings, and gluteus maximus.

Dead lifts come next. With the bar in front of you and your legs straight, bend at the waist and let the bar hang from your arms. When the bar is just off the floor, straighten up, using only your back. This will work your lower back.

After 10 dead lifts comes the military press. Start with the bar at your shoulders, wrists bent, and push up. Bring the bar down below your chin, then push up again. The military press works your pectorals and biceps.

Finally, do 10 curls. You can either keep the same grip (palms toward your body) you've been using throughout the drill and do "French curls," or reverse the grip for the more common curls. Whichever grip you choose, start with the bar at your waist and lift it to your chest, bending your arms at the elbows and keeping them right against the sides of your body. French curls will work the triceps and forearm muscles, while the regular curls work your biceps. These exercises represent the full drill and should be completed in 22 minutes.

After you've worked your way up to six full cycles, start paying attention to the time. If you can run through the whole drill in less than 22 minutes, it's time to increase the weight. Add weight in small increments, no more than 5 pounds at a time, so that you don't strain yourself. The 22-Minute Drill is hard work, but doing it regularly will make any endurance row you plan that much easier.

Ergometers

Finally there is the ergometer, the machine rowers love to hate. I don't know any rowers who really enjoy regularly working out on an ergo, but sometimes it's a necessary evil. If you live in a cold climate, sometimes an ergo is the only thing standing between you and slothfulness. Please note that I'm talking about true ergometers, not so-called rowing machines. There are dozens of rowing machines on the market, some available for as little as $70. I'm sure some are quite good, but I don't know of any that reproduce the true rowing stroke as well as the ergometers. The two best known are the units by Coffey and Concept II. Serious exercise machines designed for hard use, both these units sell for over $600. Before you begin even to think about owning an ergo, find one at a gym or rowing club and try it out. Don't just sit on it for 5 minutes, put in some time over the course of a week or two. You won't want to spend hundreds of dollars on one of these machines only to discover you hate it.

Both the Concept II and Coffey machines have electronic readouts to monitor your workout. They can be preprogrammed for a variety of different workouts. One of the biggest advantages the ergometer offers to the endurance rower, cruiser, or racer is the stroke count on the electronic readout. Once you've rowed and figured out exactly what the right stroke rate is for you and your boat to efficiently cover the most distance, you can duplicate it in your workouts. In a very short time, you can train yourself to row an hour at a time without varying your stroke

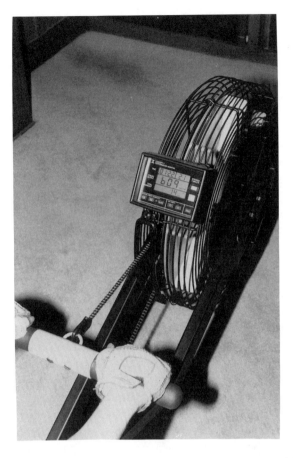

The electronic readout and enclosed flywheel of a modern ergometer. The rower has been rowing for 1 minute 22 seconds at a rate of 21 strokes per minute and an output of 609 calories per hour. She has already burned up 14 calories. This particular unit can also provide readouts on watts and distance and can be set for a variety of preprogrammed workouts.

rate by more than one stroke per minute with a consistent energy output. Of course, this doesn't take into account chop or wind, but it's a great way to teach yourself the proper rhythm and feel of rowing. Listed in the Suggestions for Further Reading is a book on the use of these machines that recommends a variety of different workouts.

No matter what you do to stay in shape, complementing your exercise program with a good diet will pay great dividends. This is not the place for a discussion of diet, but there are many books on the market written by specialists in sports nutrition. Discuss your plans with your doctor, research the available literature, and find one that suits your needs.

Five Approaches to Training

Theory is all well and good, but practice is what will make you a better, more capable endurance rower. Gordie Nash, Chris Maas, Bob Jarvis, Shirwin Smith, and Karen Carlson, all endurance rowers with impressive credentials, have kindly consented to share some of their training secrets. These are regimens of dedicated racers, but the cruiser can learn from them, too.

Gordie Nash

Gordie Nash started rowing competitively in 1978. Since that time he has won virtually every open-water race on both coasts, setting course records in many. Nash and his rowing partner, Kevin Strain, set out to win the Catalina to Marina del Rey race as their long-term goal when they paired up in early 1986. They started training for the October race in the beginning of February. Their base was Nash's houseboat in Sausalito, California, on the western shore of Richardson's Bay, a large indentation on the northern side of San Francisco Bay. Rowing the 30-foot double Nash had been designing and building for six months, they started with a route that took them around Angel Island—a trip of 10 nautical miles, which, depending upon the current, they completed in 1 hour 25 minutes. Nash figures the total workout took "about 1 hour 30 or 35 minutes, because you've got to row out there, warm up, row around the island, and warm down."

With their goal being to win the Catalina race and set a new record (see Chapter 11), speed was as important to them as endurance. Their idea was to "get the boat up to its cruising speed, or a little higher, and the next day go a little faster." Each day, they tried to improve both the boat's performance and their own physical performance by "a little bit." Their purpose was not to "try to go out there and blast around the island, but to get the heart rate and the boat's performance where we wanted them."

They rowed six days a week, with no set schedule of days off, but as they neared the racing season they planned to take the day before a race as their rest day. If there was no race on a given weekend, they made their Sunday row last 2 or 2¹/₂ hours. Nash kept a rowing journal in which he noted distance rowed, length of time, average speed, weather conditions, data from the heart-rate meters they wore, modifications to the boat, and any other information he felt was important. In addition to serving as training log and a record of the changes made to the boat, the journal provided them with clear indications of the boat's and their own potential performance under specific conditions. With this record, they could monitor their progress over the course of the year.

Nash and Strain debuted the prototype Pacific 30 in San Diego's Bay to Bay Race. They won that race averaging 7.1 knots. Two months later, after a few changes in the boat and almost 60 days of additional training, they averaged nearly 8 knots when they won the Lake Tahoe North Shore Rowing Regatta.

Before the Catalina race, Nash and Strain decided they "wanted to row a little bit more," so they added Alcatraz to their daily circuit, increasing the total to nearly 15 nautical miles, or "1 hour 58 minutes." If the weather was extremely bad, they had an alternative course through Raccoon Strait (between Tiburon and Angel Island) and into San Pablo Bay, the northern arm of San Francisco Bay. Nash remembers the summer of 1986 in San Francisco as being "pretty rough. Even at six o'clock in the morning it was blowing at least 12, 14 knots, cold and wet." Their alternative course did not provide totally smooth conditions; Raccoon Strait can be the home of some vicious, steep chop when the wind is blowing against the tide. It is rough enough so that Shirwin Smith, owner of Open Water Rowing in Sausalito, uses the area for her rough-water rowing clinics.

Two or three days a week, they augmented their rowing workouts with trips to the gym, though Nash admits, "Kevin is more religious about working with weights than I am." Their workout was complemented with a high complex-carbohydrate diet (such as fresh pasta), which included "up to, but not over, 100 grams of protein per day." They shunned "alcohol, cigarettes, drugs, and big heavy steaks."

Nash knows that not everyone has the time or the inclination to train in this way, but says, "You don't have to do that. What we were doing was pushing ourselves and the boat above our real potential, and to do that you need an incredible amount of power. To go that extra two percent, you really have to work, and we were into that range. We pushed it more than anyone else realistically would or needs to, but that's what we wanted to do. We wanted to shatter that record and make it so it would stay for years. Rob Jackson and John Aranson [who also rowed a Pacific 30 in the 1986 Catalina Race] did it 8 minutes slower. Of course, they're 10 years younger than we are, but they only trained an hour or so a day, three days a week. I think they could do it because they're excellent oarsmen who row well together and live clean healthy lives, working outdoors in physically demanding jobs. You don't really need to do 2 hours a day to row competitively in open water, but you do have to know the boat and the conditions. If you're an excellent oarsman in decent condition, you're going to do well."

Gordie Nash, who has been at the forefront of building fast, open-water rowing boats, firmly believes the sport has reached a point where the condition of the oarsman is the deciding factor. There are now enough good, proven designs available—boats like the Pacifics, the Maases, and the J-Shells—so that anyone who is serious about his racing can own a state-of-the-art open-water boat. The race is now fought by the rowers, the human engines, not by the designers. Nash says, "We're not racing Alden singles against Vancouver 21s anymore. You could put the biggest engine in the Alden and a good engine in a Vancouver, and there's no contest—the Vancouver is just that much better a boat. But you take two excellent oarsmen and put them in one of Chris's (Maas) boats and one of mine, and you're going to have a horse race." The message is clear, you can no longer make up for your own lack of condition by going out and buying the latest, fastest design. When you go to a race today, you see that everybody who wants to do well has a top-of-the-line boat under him. The only place left for improvement is in the rower.

Chris Maas

Chris Maas is the owner of the Maas Boat Company; designer and builder of the Aero, Vancouver 21, and Dragonfly; and a

Designer and builder Chris Maas rowing an Aero at Lake Tahoe. Typical of the modern, high-performance, open-water shells, the Aero (21 feet 3 inches by 25 inches by 40 pounds) is stripped down to the essentials and built for speed.

very competitive racer with a long string of wins to his record. He keeps in shape during the winter by riding his bike 6 hours a week and spending 1 1/2 hours working with free weights on a high-repetition, low-weight program. The only rowing he does during that time is boat and equipment testing.

As it gets closer to the first regatta of the season, Maas switches into his race-training mode. This consists of a regimen of 13 hours a week on his bike, 4 hours a week on his sailboard, which he considers "a really good workout if it's windy," and 6 hours of rowing. His rowing time is broken down as follows: 1 hour of interval training; 1 hour of slow rowing, perfecting his technique; 3 hours of hard rowing; and 1 hour of boat and equipment testing. As far as his diet is concerned, Maas says, "I eat everything and plenty of it," but he doesn't smoke and rarely drinks.

After his cruise in the Pacific Northwest, Maas developed some interesting insights into the type of training one might undertake before going on an extended cruise. Assuming the rower was in relatively good shape, someone who rowed 1 to 1½ hours three times a week, Maas thought that training should begin two months before the intended departure date. He feels that the hardest part about cruising is soreness. "Your butt gets sore, your hands get sore, your back gets sore." Therefore, it is necessary to condition the body to long periods of time in the boat. Maas says the best way to do that is "long rows. They don't have to be done at a fast pace. You don't have to be strong [to cruise], you just have to be conditioned to spending long periods of time in the boat."

Bob Jarvis

To many, it seems that Bob Jarvis burst on the racing scene in 1985. In fact, Jarvis had been a competitive sculler all through school. He was training for the 1968 Olympic trials when he was drafted, which put an end to his rowing for some time. Nearly 20 years later, fearing the approach of middle age, Jarvis bought himself a Pocock shell and went back to rowing. His waters were a reservoir in Los Gatos, home of the San Jose Rowing Club, just over the mountain from his home in Santa Cruz. When the reservoir went dry, Jarvis bought a Graham to row in the ocean. He came in just behind Gordie Nash in his first race, the 26-mile Monterey to Santa Cruz race. One open-water race, and he was hooked. That first season, still rowing the Graham, he tackled the Catalina race and finished a respectable third, behind Per Hertig and Gordie Nash. Since that first season, he has taken over building the Robinson/Knect (renaming it the J-Shell) and won the first six races he entered with the boat.

When he first returned to rowing, he changed his lifestyle and diet. Jarvis's diet now consists of "about 70 percent complex carbohydrates, no more than 15 percent protein, and no processed sugars." He trains five days a week on flat water, following the National Team program, which emphasizes interval and short race workouts. On the sixth day, he will do a long-distance ocean row of approximately 15 miles. For all his training and diet, Jarvis feels that "at least 70 percent of this is mental." He

Shirwin Smith, Hillary Dembroff, and Dolly Stockman rowing the Small Craft Double, modified for them by Gordie Nash, in the 1985 Catalina to Marina del Rey race.

uses visualization technique extensively and works hard at preparing himself mentally for the pain demanded to win a rowing race.

Shirwin Smith

Shirwin Smith, founder of Open Water Rowing in Sausalito, California, rowed when she was a child, then drifted away from the sport, only to come back to it more strongly. In 1984, her first year of competitive rowing, she entered the Catalina race aboard Gordie Nash's stretched Alden Double, rigged as a triple. With her were Karen "KC" Carlson and Hillary Dembroff. The following year, she rowed the race in the Small Craft Double that Nash had turned into a triple. Since her triple days, she and partner Hillary Dembroff have bought a Maas Dragonfly Double and entered selected races, regularly winning or placing high. In 1986, they won their class (women's doubles) in both the Tahoe and Great Cross Sound races.

Shirwin Smith rowing a Vancouver 21. The difference between the Vancouver and the Aero is the splash box and the 7 pounds it adds.

Before she got back into rowing, Shirwin worked for the Parks Service, where she had to meet the physical requirements to be on the fire-fighting crew. While she was with the Parks Service, she ran, "because you're out in the boonies and you have to do something with yourself." When she returned to rowing, she found she was on the water four to five days a week. Shirwin won the first short race she entered and started training on a regular basis.

Currently, she weight-trains on alternate days, using Nautilus machines and free weights for her upper body, and "rows a lot." Shirwin considers "rowing a lot" to be "at least five days a week, at least 4 miles a day and preferably 8, along with one long row, not counting teaching time. Teaching isn't training, it's paddling. When we were planning for a long race, we would do one long row a weekend. If we're planning for a 20- or 25-mile race, at least three weeks before that we would be prepared every weekend to do between 15 and 20 miles. Then, when the race came, it was just one more long row."

Recently, Shirwin went to the same nutritionist who helped Gordie Nash develop his diet and was pleased to learn that her diet was basically sound. Shirwin says, "I eat a lot of carbohydrates, a lot of breads and grain cereals, fresh vegetables and fresh fruits, a lot of dairy products, especially cheese, and fish or chicken three or four times a week. I can't eat rich things, I feel lousy afterwards. I don't smoke and only have an occasional glass of wine." Shirwin claims she is not disciplined about her diet, that she "eats what my body wants me to eat."

Karen "KC" Carlson

Karen "KC" Carlson, owner of Santa Cruz Rowing School, where she teaches ocean rowing, has been competing in women's multiple-crewed boats for several years. Nineteen eighty-six was her third Catalina race. Though fiercely competitive (no one could rack up a record like hers without being competitive), KC says, "We're not as hard-core as Gordie and Bob and some of the other men. For me, rowing still has to be fun." Fun or no fun, KC works hard at her sport. In 1984, she was stroke in the Alden Double that Gordie Nash stretched and turned into a triple for her, Shirwin Smith, and Hillary Dembroff. In 1985 and 1986, KC teamed with Linda Locklin to row doubles—first a Small Craft, then one of Chris Maas's new Dragonflies.

The first race on their schedule each year is the 26-mile Monterey to Santa Cruz race at the end of July. With Catalina as their "long-term goal," they start their "serious, planned training" for the Santa Cruz race 8 to 10 weeks before the event. KC says, "I used to just think I'd row and row and that would be enough, but I've found I need to train with weights to get stronger. I reach a point with rowing where I just don't get any better. To go faster, I have to gain strength, not endurance. On the other hand, Linda doesn't lift weights, she swims and runs." As a rowing teacher, KC finds herself in a boat "six or seven days a week, 3 to 4 hours a day," but, as Shirwin, she doesn't consider that serious training. As a team, she and Locklin try to row four days a week, varying the rowing between two 15-mile and two shorter rows. They don't row with electronics such as Strokecoaches or knotmeters, but keep accurate records of their times. By the time they've completed the Monterey to Santa Cruz race they know what kind of time to aim for at Catalina.

After the Santa Cruz race, still with an eye on Catalina, they go into maintenance training. In September there are races every weekend, and KC says, "We start to try to rest in September. We cut back some because the races take so much effort, and we figure the racing will keep us in shape. We tend to concentrate on our strategy and assessing our competition. Once September starts, I don't lift weights anymore."

On the subject of diet, KC says that "hanging around gyms makes me think more about what I eat, but being a woman and having diets shoved at you all your life, I resent diets. I do take quite a few supplements, and if I do change my diet naturally, that's fine. I think I tend to have a better diet now than I used to."

Five successful open-water racers with five different paths to success. I can contribute one more rowing program to this list—my own. When I decided to cruise the Santa Barbara Channel Islands, I looked at my rowing program to see what changes needed to be made. I'm a little different from Nash, Jarvis, Maas, Shirwin, and KC in that I'm not competitive. I row simply because I love the sport, the feeling of peace it gives me, and the places it takes me to. I rarely compete.

Before the Channel Islands cruise, I was rowing about an hour a day, six days a week. My diet was nothing special, but I eat very few sweets, and I don't smoke or drink. I didn't make any conscious changes in my diet, though I noticed I was eating less fats and more fruits the longer I trained. To increase my stamina, each week I stretched one day's row to 2^1/2 hours. Depending upon sea conditions, this meant about 15 to 18 miles. I made one mistake in this training, because I was lucky enough to have access to two boats at the time, an Aero and my Appledore Pod. I did all my training in the Aero simply because it was easier to move around. When I started the cruise aboard the fully laden

Appledore, I felt as if I were rowing a barge. For all subsequent cruises, I have always rowed the cruising boat on at least half the training rows.

You can make rowing what you want it to be. There are no absolutes in training. If you want to race or cruise, experiment with some of the methods proposed in this chapter, find out what works best for you, and put your mind to it. Remember to use the stepping-stone approach, set yourself a long-term goal, and reward yourself when you attain interim goals.

Chapter Five

Choosing a Cruising Ground

Your boat is modified, you know what to take with you, and you're in good shape. What's next? If you're a racer, it's simple; you'll go where the race organizers send you. If you're a cruiser, you have to make a decision. Actually, you have to make two decisions. You must first ask yourself if you want to cruise or make a long-distance passage. The emphasis in a long-distance passage is on getting from point A to point B, without too much concern for the sights along the way. The emphasis in cruising is more on exploration and enjoyment. A long passage is something of an endurance test; a cruise is a more leisurely affair. Once you have established which kind of trip suits you best, you must next decide where to go. This is your chance to explore intriguing bodies of water you may have read or heard about.

The most common complaint I've heard from cruisers who feel they have failed (and this applies equally to those who have attempted long passages and have had to cut their trips short) is that they tried to tackle too much too soon. Remember the stepping-stone approach to long-distance rowing. If you've never tackled an overnighter in your boat, it is probably not wise to set your sights on a 100-miler as your first cruise. Keep the 100-miler as your long-term goal, but try one or two shorter cruises or passages first.

Your first cruise can be as simple as spending a day in the boat. This is an ideal first stepping-stone. You probably won't have to make many modifications to your boat or assemble much gear. Pack some dry clothes, and think about other gear you'll want, such as an anchor, safety equipment, and provisions—a lunch and some water. Then take your boat out for a long day. You might want to row up or down the coast or lakeshore, making your goal a particular cove or point. Have lunch at your destination and row back. This first day cruise can teach you quite a bit about yourself and your boat, and it will probably whet your appetite for longer cruises.

If you've opted to challenge yourself with a long passage, you will find it easier to plan than a cruise. You may be able to start from your local area. A round trip is nice, say, 20 to 30 miles out and back, because you don't need to cope with the logistics of getting yourself and the boat home from your destination. A friend's first long-distance row was up and down the length of Lake Tahoe. The lake is 26 miles long. He took provisions for two days, rowed from the north shore to the south shore on the first day, camped out overnight, then rowed back the second day. He rowed over 50 miles and ended up right back where he started. On the other hand, it may be more psychologically rewarding to go only one way and end up farther from where you started. Take into account the amount of time you have and the area in which you plan to row.

If you are choosing a cruising ground close to home, you may already know quite a bit about it, but some aspects must be considered from the rower's perspective. It is one thing to contemplate the beauty of a coastline or lakeshore from a speeding powerboat or a well-equipped sailing boat, or even from the road. It is quite another to row along that same shore. Have you considered currents, tides, surf, beaches where you can land, wind, fog, and the locations of bottoms with good holding ground for anchoring? To be on the safe side, do all the research you would do if you knew nothing of the territory. What you learn will surprise you and also spare you some problems during the cruise or passage.

If you choose an appealing cruising area farther afield, you will need to learn what kind of weather conditions you are likely to encounter. Casual tidbits such as "Oh, it's nice there that time of year, you'll love it," won't suffice. What may be nice for a tourist staying in a hotel may not be as nice for the oarsman sleeping in his boat. Dense night and morning fogs may slip the mind of the tourist with a comfortable bed in a heated room, but the same conditions could make your trip cold, damp, and dangerous.

You will need to know about the range of temperatures, average rainfall, and force and direction of the winds. You will also need to know about the strength and extreme ranges of the tides, force and direction of the currents, direction of the surf, and a dozen other details. When you want to find out about a location, talk to those who have been there, boaters who have cruised the area. Unless they too are rowers, remember the differences between their boats and yours. If you don't know many people who have traveled your intended course, and even if you know hundreds, supplement what they tell you by further readings of your own. Find and read the local and regional boating magazines and newspapers, and, most important, an authoritative, up-to-date cruising guide.

Good cruising guides are marvelous books. They will provide you with just about everything you need to know about an area. They are full of small charts, photographs of natural and manmade landmarks, and information about weather, currents, and tides. Harbors and marinas and their entrances are described in great detail. You will learn about the history of the area, and that can add considerably to your enjoyment of a cruise. The authors' personal observations can be very helpful; some of their anecdotes make important points. A cruising guide will inform you about subjects as diverse as holding ground for anchoring and seasonal storms. Before I went to the Santa Barbara Channel Islands, I remember reading in my cruising guide, "Anacapa is suicidal in a strong Santa Ana wind." That was a bit of information that stayed with me through the cruise, and I listened very carefully to my radio for the slightest mention of the strong desert winds.

There are two factors to consider before memorizing your cruising guide. First, things change, so check your book's publication date. What was true in 1978 may no longer be true in 1988.

Second, cruising guides are written for sailors and powerboaters, not rowers. You may need to read between the lines occasionally, because there is a big difference between pushing the throttle forward half an inch to deal with an adverse current and trying to row against it. Cruising guides are available through ships' chandlers and marine bookstores, many of which offer mail-order service.

Collect and read everything you can about your chosen cruising ground. You'll want to know if the month you have chosen is the height of the mosquito season. Consult a tide table: some areas experience extremely high and low tides at certain times of the year. A beach that may be dry 11 months out of the year could be completely submerged when you choose to land there.

For your cruise you will need to know about natural and manmade sources of water. For instance, when Chris Maas and Greg Shell cruised the Pacific Northwest, they discovered scores of freshwater streams. When I cruised the Santa Barbara Channel Islands, there was no fresh water at all. It is one thing to start a cruise with three gallons of water you don't need and quite another to arrive at a deserted, dry landfall with none.

If, during your investigations into the chosen area, you begin to find major obstacles to your cruise or passage, think about changing areas. Don't become obsessed with a first-choice destination. Don't be afraid to change your mind. Even if you've already arranged to take time off from work, if your first choice turns out to be unworkable, choose another area. There are so many interesting places to cruise that you will surely be able to find a more appropriate destination. Remember, you can always go back to your first choice at some other time. Especially for a first cruise or long passage, choose a location that looks friendly.

When you look at charts of your intended cruising ground or of the area you will be passing through on an endurance row, plan for contingencies. Make careful note of beaches where you could haul out in an emergency, and towns or marinas where you might be able to pick up emergency supplies. Look also for several places where you could cut your trip short. Even if you don't have to use them, you will be more comfortable knowing you have them. In the Introduction, I mentioned that Gordie

Nash had completed only one of his three round-trip attempts from San Francisco to the Farallons and that he said, "You learn more from the ones you don't make." If you quit your trip early, remember why you stopped and use that knowledge on your next attempt.

Kyle and Suzy Collins of Salt Lake City, Utah, have approached cruising in a different, and fascinating, way. They have a 17-foot, 95-pound, WEST System, fixed-thwart Gunning Dory, which they carry on top of their 4-wheel-drive pickup truck. They load the bed of the truck with camping gear and head for Mexico and Baja California. Whenever they find an appealing beach or cove, they unload the dory, shift the camping gear to the boat, and go rowing.

The truck gives them the freedom to explore a lot of territory and cruise only those areas that interest them most. On their last three-week trip, after seeing some of the mainland coast and exploring the coves between San Jose del Cabo and Cabo San Lucas, they ended up with a four-day row through Bahia de la Concepcion. They loved the bay's wonderful beaches, spectacular scenery, and fishing, and plan to return again for a longer cruise in a larger boat they are now building.

If you don't want to make modifications to your boat or do all the planning a cruise requires, there is a new option you might want to consider: preplanned rowing excursions. In England, you can rent a traditional Thames skiff, fully equipped with camping gear, and spend several days rowing the historic river. The same type of service is being offered in Germany; in Baja California, there are planned group tours led in sailing-rowing Drascombs. Small businesses like this are sure to come and go, but they offer an alternative to doing everything yourself. A few offer the security of a group and an experienced leader. Look into them—one of them could be an ideal first rowing cruise for you.

Chapter Six

Equipment and Preparation for the Endurance Rower

When you begin planning an endurance row, there are several factors that will determine what you take: the length and duration of your journey, the area in which you intend to cruise, the availability of supplies along the way, the reliability of your boat, and your own wants and needs. The nature of your trip and the size of your boat will impose further restrictions on the gear you take along.

Preparing to Race

If you're racing, your decisions may seem deceptively easy. If you watch experienced racers, it might appear that for a race of up to 20 miles, you just have to grab a water bottle or two, get in the boat, and go. It's not quite that simple. Seasoned racers will have made many decisions and prepared thoroughly before they get to the launching area.

The racer's car or truck usually carries a complete selection of spare parts and all the tools he might need. It is amazing how a boat that has been rowed four or five days a week for a month with no gear failures will fall apart at race time. If you want to race, plan to take to the launching area all the tools you need to adjust or fix the oarlocks, foot stretchers, buttons, and riggers.

83

You will need the proper wrench or screwdriver to tighten anything on the boat that could possibly come loose. Spare nuts, bolts, or screws will come in handy if you drop something. Remember one of Murphy's laws: you will lose or break the only part for which you don't have a spare. Bring extra shims or a pitch gauge for your adjustable oarlocks and a spare fin. You will need a lubricant such as Trifalon for your sleeves. If you want a seat pad, bring one with you. Don't forget the endurance racer's best friend, duct tape. You can never have too much of this versatile commodity.

Weather and water conditions will dictate how a racer prepares for an event. If the race is scheduled to start early, it may be cold. He will therefore want to layer his upper body, making sure the clothes he chooses are comfortable to row in and easy to remove as the weather gets warmer. If it is hot and sunny, a sunscreen, preferably waterproof, may be called for. Some rowers like to wear sunglasses; others prefer a hat or a headband. If it is hot, or expected to get hot, one water bottle might not be enough. Dehydration is a great danger in competitive rowing, so if you are going to miscalculate the amount of water you carry, err on the side of caution. Most short and middle-distance races are so competitive today that no one can afford the time to stop and eat, but a few racers bring a banana or something similar for a quick boost.

Whatever the weather, the oarsman comes into contact with his boat in three places: at the oars, the footrest, and the seat. Some rowers never wear gloves, because they can't "feel" the oars as well. Some wear fingerless sailing gloves that have leather palms for protection and net backs for ventilation. Others tape their hands with masking or adhesive tape. Many rowers row barefoot all the time. Others keep a pair of warm, dry socks to slip into once they are aboard the boat.

A seat pad is also a matter of individual preference. Some people won't row without one, others can't stand them. Don't wait for the start of a race to decide whether you want the pad or not. You need to have rowed many miles both with and without one before reaching a decision. Should you suddenly decide you need a seat pad at the start of a race, you would have to find one and then reset your oarlocks to accommodate the extra height of the seat. If you have been using a pad and decide you don't need it in the race, you will have to remember to drop the height of your oarlocks.

Weather conditions will also dictate how you tune your boat for the race. If it is flat calm and predicted to stay that way throughout the day, you will want to set your oarlocks low and use a small fin for less drag. If it is rough or the local forecast says it is going to get rough, you will want to raise your oarlocks to get some extra clearance and use a larger fin for improved tracking. Tune your boat for the worst conditions you expect to encounter. It's easier to row a boat with high oarlocks and a large fin in smooth water than it is to row a boat rigged for calm conditions when the water acts up.

More and more race organizers are requiring that a personal flotation device be carried aboard each boat. You should have one with you and know how to attach it to your boat. If you are rowing a traditional design, there's no problem: just toss it aboard. If you have a brand new Aero or J-Shell, you had better figure out how you are going to carry a life preserver before the start of a race. Many rowers duct tape theirs to the deck, aft of the cockpit; others drill small holes in the hull-to-deck-joint lip aft, run a shock cord across the deck, and slip it under that. Taping on a life preserver at the last minute is one thing, but drilling holes and running shock cord can be far more time-consuming than it sounds.

By the time you've trained and are ready for your first distance race, you should know what clothes and equipment you'll need for different conditions and have these items on hand. You will have enough to do checking the boat, the course, and weather conditions (and controlling the jitters) before the start of the race without having to scrounge an extra water bottle or a life preserver and then figure out how to store it.

Some seasoned oarsmen have had terrible experiences because they weren't properly prepared at the start of a race. I remember a boatbuilder dashing about before the start of a 20-miler, trying to borrow a seat pad. He ended up being a minute or two late for his start and did very poorly in the race.

Another racer ordered a brand-new boat to be delivered at the site of a 10-mile race. The builder delivered the boat ready to race; even the oarlocks were properly pitched. The oarsman, who had been training daily, arrived with his oars. The oar buttons were set, and the oarlock height and stretchers were adjusted. The oarsman should have been able to finish well up in the fleet. He was in shape, he had a brand-new boat. Everything was going his way, except that the boat he had been training in had track shoes instead of clogs, and he was in the habit of rowing barefoot. The new boat came equipped with leather clogs and plastic heel cups. The new leather was extremely stiff. The oarsman, who had never worn socks to row, hadn't even thought of bringing a pair. He got off to a good start and soon found himself passing boats, but after 2 miles the stiff leather and hard plastic had rubbed large blisters on the sides of his feet, the tops of his toes, and on his heels. By the first turning mark, 2²/₃ miles into the race, the blisters were beginning to weep. On the next leg, the blisters tore open. The unfortunate oarsman finally had to stop because the leather was chafing the raw skin underneath. When he returned to shore, with his feet out of the clogs, the bottom of the cockpit was red with blood.

Experienced racers show up for the start of a race with far more gear than anyone could possibly imagine they would need. Gordie Nash always seems to have enough equipment to build a spare boat, and he probably does. Bob Jarvis knows what it takes to get ready for an endurance race. If he had not been properly prepared, he probably would not have made the start of the 1986 Catalina to Marina del Rey race. After carrying his boat thousands of miles on the roof of his car without incident, the seat blew out while he was on his way from Santa Cruz to Marina del Rey. Working in the California Yacht Club's parking lot, Jarvis repaired his boat while other competitors dashed to marine hardware stores searching for the lights that the event organizers had required. Serious racers are always ready to deal with the unexpected.

If you are planning a long-distance passage, you will probably need more gear than the racer, but less than the cruiser. The area you have chosen to row in and the length of your row will determine what you take with you, but you should always plan for a worst-case scenario. This is not paranoia, merely reasonable caution. The shorter the distance, the more your gear will resemble that of the racer. The longer the distance, the more it will resemble that of the cruiser. Again, your choice of boat determines the general outlines of what you can and cannot take with you.

Preparing To Cruise

When you start to prepare for a long distance-passage or cruise, you learn quickly that there is very little on the market made with the rower in mind. This doesn't mean there aren't lots of usable items, only that they weren't made for rowing. You will have to turn to other sports for the kind of gear you need. Powerboating and sailing offer some useful equipment, as do canoeing and kayaking; but nonaquatic sports such as bicycling, camping, and mountain climbing are also good sources of gear and provisions.

Since many of the items that an oarsman takes on a longer passage are matters of personal preference, I cannot make specific recommendations applicable in all situations. The suggestions that follow are intended to provide general points of reference for endurance rowers planning an extended passage.

The first thing to do after you've chosen your cruising area is to learn about it. A place close to home is easier to research, of course. If you've decided to cartop or trailer your boat to some distant lake or shore, you'll have to work a little harder. See Chapter 5 for how to go about investigating your cruising ground.

Some oarsmen leave nothing to chance. Part of the challenge of the cruise for them is anticipating every possible contingency. Others feel it is a waste of energy to lug supplies for an entire trip, knowing they can resupply en route. There is nothing wrong with stopping at a marina and buying a few supplies, but if you arrive the day the store is closed, you may be out of luck. Whether or not you choose to carry all your supplies, mark on your chart the locations of all possible resupply points.

Clothing

Once you have thoroughly researched your cruising ground and determined the capacity of your boat, it is time to consider the question of clothing. Take into account your skin type, your level of tolerance for heat and cold, and the expected weather conditions for your trip as you read the following paragraphs. No one company will be able to supply all your needs, so be prepared to think eclectically.

In some areas, you can get away with very little; in others, you will have to plan for a variety of contingencies. When I cruised the Channel Islands in late summer, I took a good hat, two T-shirts, two pairs of shorts, a light jacket, and shoes for going ashore. This would be appropriate attire in that area six or seven months out of the year. In the middle of winter (yes, there is winter in Southern California), I would add a pair of long sweatpants, a heavier jacket or vest, a heavier shirt, and some rain gear.

Clothes for endurance rowing should be functional and comfortable. There are a lot of clothes that you just can't row in. Slash or kangaroo pockets on sweatshirts and jackets—unless they can be closed with zippers, snaps, or Velcro—can trap your thumbs when you push your hands away from your body at the start of the recovery. Some rowers solve this problem by wearing their sweatshirts inside out or backward, but this tends to make the hood, if any, less wearable. Find sweatshirts without pockets, or remove them. Rugby shirts are a great alternative to the sweatshirt, although they have no hood. I know one oarsman who rows in bicycling jerseys because he likes the pockets they have built into the back. A good oiled sailing sweater is warm, but it is bulky for the protection it provides, can be itchy, usually needs special care, and may take a long time to dry.

A good jacket for rowing should be neither too loose nor too tight. Your best bet for finding the right jacket will be the catalogs of camping and mountain-climbing equipment manufacturers. After searching far and wide, I have settled on a vest rather than a jacket. My vest happens to be made by Patagonia. It has a flat, unquilted nylon shell and a high-tech pile the company calls

Synchilla. It is tough, lightweight, and water-resistant. When it does get wet, it dries quickly. The large armholes do not restrict my movements while I am rowing, and the two slash pockets can be closed with heavy plastic zippers. This vest was not designed for extreme conditions, but it works well for me. I usually wear it unzipped, layering underneath with a T-shirt and a rugby jersey for added warmth. When I buy a new vest, I will look for one with a longer tail flap to protect the small of my back at the catch. In general, avoid front pouches, loose pockets, draw-strings, and long flaps that could catch in your tracks or under your wheels. The few rowing jackets on the market are designed more for training than the long passage, but take a look at them anyway; you might find one just right for you. Float Coats are a specialty item that we will discuss in Chapter 8, "Safety and First Aid."

As with sweatshirts, the pockets of shorts can cause problems. I once had a great pair of baggy nylon shorts. They would have been perfect for rowing—the seams didn't chafe, they dried almost instantly, they didn't bind the legs—but they had big front pockets that ballooned out just waiting to catch my thumbs. I have recently discovered shorts made by a company called Big Dogs, whose slash pockets close with snaps. So far the snaps haven't rusted out in salt water. Many endurance rowers wear bicycling or rowing shorts. You might want to consider running or gym shorts if you are going to be cruising in a hot climate.

Some clothes are fine for daily rowing, but inappropriate for long cruises. For instance, many people wear Lycra tights for an early-morning row. They are warm and snug-fitting, so they don't snag or catch your hands. They can also become uncomfortably hot, and they are almost impossible to get off in a boat.

There is a variety of reasons you might want to change clothes as you row. You may need to take off a vest or long-sleeved shirt, or change from sweatpants to shorts as temperature rises, or slip on a jacket when the afternoon wind picks up. Make sure that you can make the change easily and safely in the confines of your boat. If you have to lie down on your living room floor to wriggle into a pair of tights, they probably aren't appropriate for a long cruise during which you may want to change.

If it's going to be extremely cold where you're rowing, look into long underwear. Most of the expedition clothiers make some, and the new stuff is as far removed from the old, red wool long johns as an Aero is from a flat-bottomed work skiff. The new long underwear is far lighter and less bulky than its predecessors. It is also more comfortable and thermally efficient. There are several different types on the market, so look at more than one before you buy.

Socks, Gloves, and Hats. Socks, gloves, and hats are all matters of personal preference. If your feet tend to get cold, by all means find some good socks. I do not recommend a quick trip to the local discount department store for a pair of gym socks. Go to a camping or mountain-climbing store and get something that really suits your purpose. Modern climbing and sports socks are made of fiber blends that wick moisture away from your feet, provide more warmth for their weight and bulk, prevent blisters, and dry quickly when they get soaked. Remember, the farther up the calf they go, the warmer they will be.

Gloves have also improved a lot lately. If you just want to prevent blisters, the same fingerless sailing gloves that racers use will do fine. If you're interested in warmth, there are some gloves made especially for rowers. Most expedition clothiers offer a variety of gloves with different features that you should check out.

Hats are a frequently overlooked necessity. On cold mornings, a good hat can help you retain vast amounts of body heat; on hot days, it can save you from baking your brain. For the cold, I recommend a good cap rather than a sweatshirt or jacket hood. The hood can block your vision when you turn; the hat turns with you. For years, I wore a standard wool watch cap. My head itched, but I was warm, and I thought an itchy head was the price you paid for warmth. Later, I was given a Patagonia cap made out of one of their high-tech fibers, and I find that it is just as warm as my old cap, but doesn't itch. My new hat is bright red. I like to think it helps other boaters see me a bit better.

If you are looking for protection from the sun rather than for warmth, there are several options. A sun visor shields your face

A wide-brimmed straw hat provides good protection from the sun. Tights are comfortable for daily rowing, but can be difficult to change out of at sea if they become too warm.

and keeps sweat out of your eyes, but does nothing to protect the top of your head, the tops of your ears, or the back of your neck. Mesh-back baseball caps provide good ventilation but don't protect you any better than visors. A full-fabric baseball cap protects the entire head, but it can get hot and doesn't protect the tops of the ears or the back of the neck. Wide-brimmed canvas or woven straw hats offer the best combination of protection and ventilation. A hat of this kind is essential to your rowing wardrobe. A light string tying the hat to a loop around your neck can save the hat from being lost overboard in a sudden gust of wind.

Layering. The key to dressing for the oarsman is layering. This technique is well known to those who live in the Northeast, where the weather can change drastically in the space of an hour. It is not as well understood by people from parts of the country where the weather is more stable. I first learned about layering on a row off Newport, Rhode Island. The weather went from a sunny 70 degrees to wind, clouds, thunder and lightning, rain, and hail, and back to sunshine, all before lunch. The idea behind layering is to carefully select several layers of light clothing appropriate for different weather conditions, and to add and subtract these as the weather changes. On a cold morning, you might put on a pair of shorts and a T-shirt, then sweatpants and a rugby shirt, with a vest, hat, and gloves as your outer layer. As it gets warmer, you start peeling clothing off. If it gets colder again, you put something back on. In this way, you avoid having to make several complete changes of clothing.

Sunglasses. If you are going to wear sunglasses, get a decent pair. The new unbreakable frames and lenses pay for themselves the first time you sit on them. A lanyard that lets you hang the glasses around your neck is a sensible precaution to take against losing your investment overboard. Most new brand-name sunglasses have some UV screen in their lenses to protect against eye damage. Keep this in mind when you buy. You could even justify the expense of good polarized lenses by treating them as safety equipment.

I learned about the safety value of good sunglasses in Mexico, when I was about to take a shortcut between the mainland and an outcropping of offshore rocks. The shortcut would have saved me almost a mile. The sun was bright, and the water shone like a sheet of beaten silver. I happened to be wearing a pair of Hobie sunglasses with polarized lenses, which allowed me to see through the reflection on the water. I discovered that the calm surface hid a tumble of boulders, some only inches from the surface.

Rain Gear. Rowers must choose their rain gear very carefully. There is a wide selection of good gear on the market, some of it for bicyclists, some of it for offshore sailors, and some for mountain climbers. There is none made specifically for rowers. Good rain gear that suits the oarsman's purpose is not easy to find. The fixed-thwart rower definitely has the advantage in this department. Most rainwear is either too heavy and stiff to give the sliding-seat rower the freedom he needs, or too loose to stay free of the wheels of the seat. A fixed-thwart oarsman can row in a poncho or good, heavy foul-weather gear. The sliding-seat rower must balance dryness against bulk and flexibility. As with jackets, beware of slash pockets, drawstrings, and loose tail flaps.

If you are going to be rowing in heavy fog and drizzle, you can probably get away with lightweight, flexible mountain-climbing or ski gear that will keep you dry, yet still breathes. If you expect a downpour, you may have to get heavier gear. Be sure you can row in it before you buy it. Go to a good bike shop and look at some of their touring rain gear; it might just work for you. A final word on rain gear: I don't recommend hoods, because they limit your vision at a time when you can least afford it. Wrap a towel around your neck to prevent water seeping in, and use a good rain hat instead of a hood.

You don't have to go out and spend a fortune on a special rowing wardrobe all at once. When you do buy new clothing, however, keep in mind your needs as an oarsman. One final note on clothing: don't take brand-new gear on a long trip. Be sure you've rowed in everything you plan to take on a trip before you go. Twenty-five miles into a trip is not the time to find out that you can't go into the catch position in your new rain gear or that your thumbs snag in your jacket pockets each time you initiate a recovery.

Storage

No matter what clothes you decide you need, you'll want to keep them dry when you're not wearing them. If you have rowed all day in a wind-driven spray and reach camp only to discover that the warm, dry clothes you've been thinking about for the past two hours are wetter than the clothes you're wearing, you will be truly disappointed.

The weather and the type of boat you row will determine the kind of storage bag you'll use. If you row an open-water shell, you will have to use canoe or kayak bags strapped to the hull. These are very dry, but virtually impossible to get at while underway. Canoe or kayak bags can also be used aboard traditional boats and do well in extreme conditions. I used to use a body, or coroner's, bag on *Kavienga*. It had a rugged, full-length plastic zipper and was perfectly watertight. So many people told me it was "gross" and "disgusting" that I finally shifted over to a pair of small Bone Dry kayaking storage bags when the body bag wore out. The two small bags are better than the one large one because I can shift them around the boat for better weight distribution. For shorter trips in good weather, I just toss gear into a knapsack. This day pack is water-repellent and keeps everything together. Clothes are not the only gear you will be carrying that needs to be kept dry. Think about this when you contemplate adding equipment and supplies.

Kyle and Suzy Collins, who do their cruising in the Sea of Cortez where they don't have to worry about weather other than heat, pack all their extra clothing, toilet articles, provisions, and camera in four Grade IV canoe packs. These compact packs have watertight roll tops and are easy to handle. They keep their camping equipment in the self-contained bags it came in, and the bags and packs allow them to shift gear as necessary to balance the boat. With everything in watertight bags, they don't have to worry about keeping special items dry. As with clothing, the solutions to the problem of onboard storage seem to come from other sports: canoeing, kayaking, and backpacking.

Camping Equipment

Depending upon the length of your passage and the conditions you expect to encounter, you will need to carry a certain amount of camping gear. If you haven't looked at camping equipment lately, you will find the gear on the market today has come a long way. Gone are the days of heavy canvas tents and thick, heavy sleeping bags that, once wet, stay wet forever.

If you plan to be sleeping aboard, or if the climate is mild and there aren't a lot of bugs, you may not need a tent at all. It would be a shame, though, to miss out on using a modern tent; there are so many great ones available. If you are not familiar with the new models, talk to knowledgeable salespeople or campers and hikers you respect. Gather enough information to make the proper choice. Although these tents are good, they are also expensive, and you don't want to spend more than you have to.

Unless you already have one, I don't recommend the dome tents. They look high-tech and roomy, but most are designed for serious expeditions into heavy snow country. Their weight disqualifies them for the average rowing excursion. I have spent some time in an oddly shaped tent by North Face called the Bullfrog. It has netting that keeps out the bugs but lets in cool breezes and a rain flap if the weather turns nasty. It packs into a tiny space and weighs only 6 pounds. If this is too heavy for you, a new model called the Tadpole is coming out soon. It is said to weigh only 4 pounds. A company called Moss Tents also offers some interesting equipment that you might want to look into. Find a local mountaineering and backpacking specialty store, and browse their selections and catalogs.

Sleeping bags have also changed considerably in the past few years. If you have a moldy old bag in your basement or attic, you can certainly air it out and use it, as long as it is made of a synthetic material. Otherwise, look for a new sleeping bag. There is a great variety to choose from on the market. Modern sleeping bags are designed for specific conditions. You can probably find one that suits your needs within your price range.

Sleeping bags are rated according to the lowest temperature the bag can handle. Find a synthetic bag that is rated for the coldest temperature you expect to encounter. If a 20-degree bag is adequate, you will only be wasting money and burdening yourself with extra bulk by buying a bag rated to minus 10 degrees. North Face and Moonstone are both well-known brands and offer a good selection. Look for a bag that weighs between $2^1/_2$ and $3^1/_2$ pounds.

I have found that an inexpensive inflatable air mattress, which weighs very little and folds down to almost nothing, makes a critical difference in my comfort on any longer passage. It is easier to store than a foam pad, which usually has to be rolled up and kept dry. When you pack your air mattress, be sure to include a patch kit. If you don't have the patch kit with you, you'll inevitably put a hole in the mattress.

A good stove is essential. You can eat cold food straight from the can, but do you really want to? In the morning, do you want to do without a hot cup of coffee or tea? There are several excellent camping stoves that weigh very little and burn either propane or white gas. My friends who spend more time camping than I do tell me that "propane is not cost efficient" and that "white gas is the way to go."

Stay away from stoves that have to be pressurized unless you are very familiar with them. I was at Bahia de Santa Maria once, a beautiful bay 25 miles south of San Felipe on the Sea of Cortez. The bay is about a half-mile deep. Its tides are so great that the entire bay dries out at low tide. It is a wonderful place to explore, but I had to spend most of my time trying to pressurize the old Coleman stove I'd borrowed. When you are considering a stove, the features to look for are weight, fuel efficiency, and the time it takes to boil a quart of water. A company called MSR makes some good stoves that you might want to look at. Nearly all camping stoves come with a convenient little package of lightweight cooking utensils—much better than raiding your kitchen cabinets for a spare ladle and spatula.

Lights

Aside from providing light to read or eat by, lanterns are important for your safety. If you are sleeping aboard and you even suspect there may be other craft moving in your vicinity, keep a lantern lit. Aboard *Kavienga,* I place an oar upright in the mast partner and hang a lantern from it. You can achieve the same effect by resting one oar across the boat, using the oarlocks to hold it, and lashing the other to it vertically. In the interest of safety, I prefer a battery-powered lantern over one with a flame. Be sure to start your trip with a fresh battery and pack a spare along with an extra bulb.

Food

If you are going somewhere where you can count on finding fresh water, you can liberate a lot of space in your boat and lighten your load by taking freeze-dried food. It is widely available, easy to store, and usually quite tasty. If you can't count on finding fresh water, or if weight and space aren't your major concerns, the alternative is canned food.

Even if you are going to pack your cans in a watertight bag, take the time to mark each one with a grease pencil so you know what it contains. A little spray can do considerable damage to a paper label. If you are going to be out for a long time, you will want to remove the labels, mark the cans with grease pencil, and varnish them to protect them from rust, but most rowers are not on the water long enough to make this procedure necessary. Be sure to take *two* can openers. No matter what kind of food you choose, take plenty of it.

If you're out for only one night, you can get by with almost anything, but if you're planning a longer trip, make each meal a special treat. A good meal on a secluded beach after a long row is a wonderful experience. Test foods at home before you go. Take lots of snacks that you can eat easily while rowing. I like apples, bananas, dried apricots, and a variety of trail mixes while I row. Others prefer candy bars or beef jerky. You're going to burn up a lot of calories while you row, so be sure you have the means of replenishing your reserves.

If you enjoy fishing, I suggest you use your catch to supplement your diet. Don't plan your menus around what you hope to catch. One summer I rowed a beautiful mountain lake in Idaho. The water was perfectly clear, and I could see scores of large trout, but none of them would take a lure or fly. I sat in the boat eating a sandwich and watching the fish congregate in the shade of the hull.

Water

Nothing you take with you is more important than water. Rowing is exhausting and dehydrating work. Be sure you have more than enough water and that you store it carefully. A friend who rows the Sea of Cortez, where fresh water is virtually unobtainable, uses some marvelous collapsible water jugs. He likes them because he can flatten them when they're empty and store them out of the way. He has also started taking a solar still with him. This device, borrowed from liferafts, turns salt water into fresh through condensation. He carries it as a backup in case he runs into trouble and has to stay out longer than planned. He says that the water produced by the still doesn't taste great, but that it could save his life in an emergency.

I prefer to carry water in half-gallon plastic bottles, as it comes from the store. The bottles are small and easy to handle. Each one is sealed. If one has a hole, I lose the water in that one only. By distributing the bottles around the boat, I can balance her better. Storing the empties doesn't bother me; they can be refilled or disposed of along the way. If you have found a good anchorage and plan to use it again that day, you can tie one of your empty jugs to the anchor line to mark it and spare yourself having to hoist the anchor for a short row.

After food, clothing, and water, you still have a lot of gear to load aboard your boat: first-aid, navigation, and safety gear, all treated in later chapters; toilet articles; and dishes and eating utensils. Some people can get by with a single pan, using it for both cooking and eating. Others prefer plastic, metal, or paper plates. Some people just have to have their morning coffee in a special, insulated mug. If it makes you happy and your boat can hold it, take it.

One item that expedition outfitters can supply is a waterproof toilet paper container. You'll be glad you invested in it. Toilet articles vary from person to person, but should include moisturizing lotion.

There are a few items that you might want to add to your list of gear just for personal pleasure. A small transistor radio makes a pleasant camping companion, as does a good book. A notebook can be used as a logbook. Not only can a log be fun to keep and refer to later, it can also assist you in your cruising. Since your boat is smaller than most cruising boats, it will be more affected by shallow water, tides, localized wind patterns, and the like. Make notes of anything you encounter that affects you and add this to your charts for future reference, and check your notes on your return trip. These will all need to be stored in a dry place.

A camera is fun to have along, but requires some special care. No matter how good your watertight storage bags are, I would not recommend bringing an expensive new camera on a rowing expedition. Take either a "disposable" camera or one of the new "sports cameras" designed to stand up to conditions around the water. I carry a Cosina aboard *Kavienga*. This small 35mm camera comes in a compact underwater housing that seems bullet-proof. If you take a camera, remember to keep your film cool. Don't let it bake all day in a sealed bag.

Tools

The racer has to bring a truckload of tools to the start of an event; the cruiser has to take his tools with him. Weight and available storage space will force the cruiser to be more selective about the tools and spare parts he takes along. If possible, find tools that have more than one use. A Crescent wrench, for instance, can take the place of several open-end or box wrenches. Don't agonize over each tool. If you think you might need it, take it. There isn't a lot to break on a rowing boat, but anything that does break can ruin your trip.

A good knife is worth its weight in gold on a boat. In fact, you should consider bringing two of them: a good, heavy, sheath knife and a smaller, more compact pocket knife. Don't scrimp on either one—a good knife will last a lifetime and serve you in many ways.

Spare Parts

If you're rowing fixed-seat, pack a spare oarlock; you never know what you might drop. If you're rowing sliding-seat, take an extra lock, its associated pin, and the nuts and washers that they require. Pins have been known to break. Be sure you have the wrench you need to remove the broken pin. Depending upon the length of your trip, you might want to take an extra sliding seat. They don't weigh much, they're easy to store, and you can't easily repair or replace one on a cruise.

In any discussion of spare parts, the question of carrying an extra oar or pair of oars always comes up. I have broken only two oars in my life, and both were snapped in the surf, but this doesn't mean I won't break a third on a cruise. I asked Chris Maas if he and Greg took spares on their cruises, and they said no. They felt the stresses of cruising would be far less than those of racing, and they had never broken an oar racing. They would also have faced the problem of storing a spare on their open-water shells. If I were contemplating a cruise in an Aero or Vancouver 21, I would also opt to leave the spare at home. When I cruise in *Kavienga,* however, I do carry a spare.

Anchors

Open-water shells don't require anchors, but they do come in handy on traditional designs. Because traditional boats are light and have low windage as compared with motorboats or sail-boats, it doesn't take much to anchor them. Your choice of anchor will depend on the size of your boat and the bottom where you most often anchor. Aboard *Kavienga,* I use a 12-pound modified mushroom (the long shaft common to these anchors was cut down to make it more manageable aboard), which works very well in sand and gravel and moderately well in rock. It is equipped with 5 feet of $3/16$-inch chain and 60 feet of $3/8$-inch nylon rode. This gear is a little heavy for a 16-foot peapod and does not conform to my minimalist principles. My excuse is that I had it left over from a small sailboat I once owned and have not been able to bring myself to go out and spend the money on lighter ground tackle. In case of an emergency, the nylon rode could be used as a towline or streamed as a warp (a long bight of line trailed behind a boat to slow its progress and keep it end-on to the seas) in heavy seas.

If you are rowing a traditional design and plan to haul out at night, think about how you will go about sliding the boat up the beach. Both sand and rock can damage the bottom of your boat. Furthermore, the boat, fully loaded, can be extremely heavy. Before you go, try moving your boat with a full load. You may want to look into rollers. There are some good inflatable rollers that take up very little space in the boat.

Once you have assembled all your clothes, food, tools, safety gear, and navigation equipment, take a long, hard look at it. Remember you will have to share the limited space in your boat with this gear and propel its weight every foot of the way through sheer muscle power. Of his long row along the Maine coast, John Garber says he started out "overloaded and over-equipped." There is a fine line between being overequipped and underequipped, one that each oarsman must draw for himself. The distinction is usually best understood in hindsight. The limits you set after your last voyage will make the preparations for your next journey that much easier. If it comes down to a choice between being "overloaded" or underequipped, err on the side of caution. It is usually easier to get rid of gear along the way (Garber reports unloading "30 pounds of redundant gear") than to acquire exactly what you need en route. I don't recommend starting out with a lot of stuff you plan to throw away, but if you have pared down to the "bare necessities" and still find you're lugging around stuff that you don't need, get rid of it.

Whether you are going out for a 20-mile race or a 100-mile cruise, once you've practiced storing all your gear, go over your boat. Examine everything, making sure it is in top working order. This is no time to procrastinate. A squeaking seat is not going to suddenly fix itself 15 miles offshore; a cross-threaded nut on an oarlock gate is not going to repair itself. If your bailer has been hard to open or close, you can be sure it won't lubricate itself on a beach 30 miles from home. Take it apart and fix it before you leave. If the thwart's varnish is lifting and there's the possibility of splinters, sand it down and apply two or three coats of good varnish. Take the time to do repairs properly, and you'll save yourself a lot of time and trouble on the water. It's always easier to make repairs at home, where you have more tools and are closer to suppliers you know and trust. When your boat slides into the water at the start of the race or cruise, you want it to be in the best condition possible.

Chapter Seven

Navigation

Whether you've chosen a long passage, cruise, or race, you will need to know how to keep track of where you are and where you're going. Many people think of navigation as an esoteric science, bordering on the occult. It's not that tough. In this chapter, we will be dealing with a few simple tools and methods of laying a course, figuring out where you are, and learning how to get where you want to go. This chapter is not designed to get you across oceans, but rather to put you at ease while making coastal passages.

Navigation technology has made remarkable advances in this century. Where we once had compass, chart, and sextant, we now have Loran, radio direction finders (RDF), and satellite navigation (SatNav). Unfortunately, you probably will not be using these modern wonders aboard your rowing boat. Actually, Loran and RDF units have been miniaturized to the point that they could be carried on a rowing boat, but for present purposes we will be discussing simpler tools of coastal navigation.

The tools we will be discussing in this chapter are the magnetic compass, dividers, parallel rulers, and charts. These should be enough to get you where you want to go safely. To these, you might want to add a pair of binoculars and, for many types of navigation, a watch with either a sweep second hand or a digital readout. Most rowing-boat navigation is rather rough; it is used merely to get you to the general vicinity of your destination. As you close on your landfall or mark, check its location visually and make any necessary alterations in course. As long as you remember to update your navigation visually, you will be fine.

Compasses

More and more rowers are buying boats with permanently mounted compasses, which have the advantage of always staying in the same place, and can't be lost. You don't have to get the most expensive compass; just be sure the one you have is easy to read from the seat or thwart. For navigational purposes, a hand-bearing compass is a great help, though not a substitute for the main compass. You can hold it to your eye and sight through it, rather than spinning your boat around and trying to take sightings from the permanent compass. John Crutchfield, who rows an Aero out of Dana Point, California, may have the best of both worlds. He has mounted a bracket for a hand-bearing compass on his stretchers. That way, he can use it both as a permanent compass and, removed from the bracket, for taking bearings.

I will not go into compensating or swinging your compass. On large ships and yachts, it is necessary to have a professional compensate your compass to remove as much of the deviation as possible, then "swing" your compass and prepare a deviation table based on errors still in the readings. These errors are usually caused by the magnetic pull of large masses of metal, such as the engine, aboard the boat. It is not practical to swing a compass on a rowing boat, since most items are not permanently fixed. Be careful when you load your boat to keep as much metal away from the compass as possible. More significant than metal will be the presence of another magnetic field, such as another compass or a radio or tape player. On some headings, your compass may still read a degree or two off, but for the kind of distance most of us row this hardly matters. These small deviations are another reason to update your navigation visually as you close on your destination.

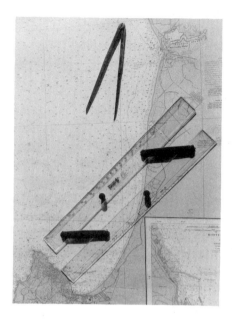

Parallel rulers and dividers,
the basic tools for navigation.

Parallel Rulers and Dividers

Along with a compass, you will need a set of parallel rulers and a pair of dividers, which can be purchased at a chandlery, marine bookstore, or marine hardware store. You will use these to lay your course and plot your position. The parallel rulers will allow you to "walk" from the compass rose to your position, and vice versa. The dividers allow you to measure distance. Be sure to take distance readings from the latitude intervals marked on the sides of your chart, rather than from the longitude intervals on the top or bottom.

Charts

Most or all of the charts you will be using are published by the National Ocean Survey. There are several types, classified roughly according to their scale. Voyage-planning, or sailing, charts cover the largest area at the smallest scale, such as 1:1,000,000 or more. An example of this type of chart is 18020, which covers the area from San Diego to Cape Mendocino at a scale of 1:1,444,000, or 20 nautical miles to the inch. There are larger-scale sailing charts inside 18020, such as 18022, which covers the area from San Francisco to Ensenada at a scale of 1:868,003, but this chart still shows very little detail. Unless you are planning to cross oceans, these charts will be of little use to you.

Next down in scale is the general chart, which covers a smaller area at a larger scale. Chart number 18740, inside charts 18020 and 18022, covers the area from San Diego north to Santa Rosa Island. Its scale is 1:234,270, or roughly 3 nautical miles to the inch. Charts with this scale show considerably more detail, but still omit important data. This type of chart will be slightly more useful to the long-distance oarsman.

The charts rowers rely on are called coastal, or coast, charts. Chart number 18765, labeled "Approaches to San Diego Bay," covers an area from just below the Coronado Islands to Solana Beach using a scale of 1:100,000, or roughly 1$1/2$ miles to the inch. This type of chart shows major landmarks clearly. You will also find buoys, kelp, and offshore rocks marked on coast charts.

Harbor charts have the largest scale and consequently the most detail. Chart number 18773 depicts San Diego Harbor and the immediate coast at a scale of 1:12,000, or 1 mile to 6$1/8$ inches. Harbor charts are perfect if you are plotting courses for training or if you wish to explore a new harbor.

You will find charts listed in Nautical Chart catalogs at chart outlets. The catalogs are well laid out, showing a large area, the various charts contained in it, and their overlaps. You can buy charts at marine hardware stores, specialty bookstores, and the like. Along with your first chart, you will need to buy National Oceanographic Survey Chart number 1, which is not a chart, but a booklet explaining symbols and abbreviations used on charts.

Once you have your chart, see if it needs correcting and updating. Correcting a chart means to bring it up to date as far as compass variation is concerned. Variation is the difference between true, or geographic, north and the magnetic north registered by the compass. The magnitude of the difference varies between widely separated locales and changes gradually with time. In the center of a compass rose on your chart, you will find local variation at the time the chart was printed, the date the chart was printed, and the annual change in variation. Usually the change is minor, 3 minutes or so; if the chart is relatively current, you won't really need to bother making any change. For instance, chart number 18685, showing Monterey Bay, had an original variation of 15 degrees 45 minutes. It was printed in 1981 and shows an annual decrease of 4 minutes. Therefore, in 1988 the total decrease is 28 minutes, hardly worthy of concern. If, however, your chart is considerably older, you will want to make the necessary corrections.

Updating a chart simply means adding the latest information to it. The Coast Guard issues its weekly "Notice to Mariners," which contains everything you need for updating. Many rowers ignore these notices and never have a problem. A friend of mine, however, made the mistake of ignoring the notice about a security zone off President Nixon's Western White House in the early 1970s. He was rowing along just outside the kelp beds when two Coast Guard boats intercepted him. He had to do some fast talking and make a long detour around the zone.

Charts are wonderful, informative, and interesting, but also large. Chart Kits and Chart Guides are smaller, cheaper, and more convenient to use. In many cases, they provide more information in almanac form than a government chart. In my opinion, they are most effective when used with, not instead of, the National Ocean Survey (NOS) charts. You can also carry a lot of information by copying appropriate pages of your cruising guide, which could even be reduced and laminated to save space and protect the paper.

Apart from being large and unwieldy, charts also have to be kept dry. They can be kept rolled in waterproof chart tubes, or folded and placed in protective bags. Waterproof charts are available, but not always easy to find. No matter how you deal with the problem of wetness, charts still require a lot of space to be rolled out. As an alternative, I would strongly recommend a practice I call "prenavigation."

Prenavigation

Prenavigation allows you to leave your charts and navigation tools at home and carry only your compass. You will be able to do your navigation at your leisure, in the comfort of your own home, long before you leave the beach. Instead of battling with a rocking boat while you try to unroll a chart, you can practice your navigation on the dining room table or living room floor.

If you are planning to race, get a copy of the course chart and copy the location of the marks onto a navigation chart. Once you have transferred the marks, use your parallel rulers to lay your course from the start to the first mark, from the first mark to the second, and so on. Be sure to use magnetic headings, not true ones, so that you'll be speaking the same language as your compass.

Most compasses on rowing boats are mounted near the foot stretchers or on the aft deck. If your compass is not a back reader, you will have to figure a reciprocal course so that, looking backward, you will be reading the course properly. This is a simple matter: If the course is over 180 degrees, subtract 180 for the reciprocal. If it is less than 180 degrees, add 180. For instance, if the course from the start to the first mark is northeast, or 45 degrees, you will need to add 180 degrees to get the course you will see on your compass, 225 degrees. Once you have the courses, you can either write them on a pad or, as I prefer to do, write them in grease pencil on your boat. When you get to the racecourse, make sure there have been no course changes. Some race committees will give you the courses to the marks. Be sure they have given you magnetic, not true, headings and, if you need to, figure the reciprocal course.

The same method of prenavigation can be used by the cruiser and the passage-maker, or even in training. If your cruise or passage is going to take you from point A to point B, simply lay out the course at home, then watch your compass as you row. You won't be able to make accurate fixes during the cruise, but most of the time that won't be necessary. If you can't go from point A to point B in a straight line—say, a point of land is blocking your way—you can treat the obstacle like the mark of a racecourse. Lay your course for a spot safely off the obstacle, then figure the course from that spot to point B. Do your reciprocals, then make a note of the two courses. A long passage or cruise can be laid out this way, plotting the course from point to point. To compensate for tides, currents, winds, and just plain sloppy rowing, you will want to check your progress visually and regularly and update your navigation as required.

Prenavigation also comes in handy in your daily training. Many rowers don't enjoy rowing the same training course day after day. Weather conditions sometimes make the regular course unattractive. Most harbors have a number of buoys offshore, both navigational and yacht-club spar buoys, all of which are fully marked and described on the local yacht club's outside course chart. This chart will even have the distances between buoys and the compass headings. Obtain a copy of the chart, lay out as many courses as you think you will need, varying their direction and length to accommodate weather conditions and your training plan, do your reciprocals, and make a list.

I have drawn five courses off my local harbor, ranging in distance from 5 to 17 miles. They all share the entrance buoy as a common starting point. Each day, when I reach the entrance buoy, I assess the weather conditions and pick the appropriate course, taking into account whether I feel like punching into a chop or riding with the wind. Not only are the compass headings and reciprocals already done, I know the distances between marks and the total length of the course, so that I can monitor my training accurately.

This prenavigation will get you from a known point A to a known point B, but it will not allow you to do much more than guess where you are between the points. Neither will it allow you to plot a course to a secondary destination. If you want to be able to determine your exact position and figure a new course from there to a new destination, you will have to carry your tools with you.

The Two-Bearing Fix

The only type of position-fixing navigation we are going to discuss here is a two-bearing fix. First, you will need to spot two easily identifiable landmarks on shore and locate them on your chart. Ideally, these landmarks will be more than 20 degrees apart. Take a reading off both with either your hand-bearing compass or your permanent one. If you are using a hand-bearing compass, you will have to figure a reciprocal. (If the bearing is more than 180 degrees, subtract 180 from it. If it is less than 180 degrees, add 180 to it.) Once you have the reciprocals, find the bearing on the magnetic compass rose and use the parallel rulers to walk the bearings back to the landmark. Draw these bearings, or lines of position (LOP), from the landmarks out to sea. Where the LOPs cross is your position. Mark the location with the time the sightings were made, and you will have a good basis for future dead reckoning. Since you haven't taken deviation into account, this position will be a little off, but it should be adequate for your purposes.

Using parallel rulers in a rowing boat is not easy, although it can be managed in rough fashion with the chart spread out on your lap. When two charted landmarks or a buoy and a landmark align, you have the opportunity for a transit, an accurate LOP that does not require use of the parallel rulers. Suppose, as you row, a lighthouse on a distant shore moves from your perspective directly behind and above a gong buoy in the middle distance. Draw a line on the chart from the lighthouse through the buoy. Your position lies along the extension of that line. Cross it with a bearing or, if you are very fortunate, another transit to get a fix.

For a rough position fix, you can use a single LOP. Your results won't be very accurate, but they may be better than nothing. If you are sure you have maintained a good course from your starting point to your destination and can only find one landmark on shore, take a reading off it and plot your LOP. Where the LOP intersects your course is your position. Be sure to label this fix as a single-bearing fix so that you will remember it is an approximate position.

Dead Reckoning

Dead reckoning is probably the most common form of navigation rowers use. In dead reckoning, one adds estimated data to known data to extrapolate an approximate position. For instance, you were able to do a two-bearing fix at noon and it is now three o'clock. If you know the course you rowed and your estimated speed, you can simply pace off the distance covered in the proper direction to develop a rough guess of your position. The by-the-book definition of dead reckoning would have you stop there, without attempting to factor the effects of current, tide, wind, or sloppy rowing, but I have always felt that when I guess at my postion, I want it to be the best guess I can muster. So correct your estimated course and distance traveled for any systematic influence you can think of, and label the resultant position clearly as a dead reckoning location so you will remember that it is approximate. Correct it with a two-bearing fix at the earliest opportunity.

There are other ways to determine position, such as running fixes, bow and beam bearings, etc. Celestial navigation is a fascinating science, but it is not necessary for the type of excursion we are concerned with. Celestial navigation, night piloting, and special navigation techniques are all described in great detail in the Suggestions for Further Reading. Most rowers navigate by sight, but if you think you are going to need more help in determining your position, I encourage you to explore navigation further.

Chapter Eight

Safety and First Aid

The solo distance rower must accept total responsibility for his own safety. During a race, there are always other competitors around you and often chase or escort boats as well, and a life preserver or personal flotation device (PFD) is usually a sufficient precaution. On a long-distance passage or a cruise, however, you are at the mercy of the elements and there is no one around to help you. Preparation, planning, and experience can help you avoid trouble, but sometimes, no matter how well prepared and careful you are, trouble will find you.

You *must* carry a PFD, not just because the Coast Guard says you have to, but because it is the single most important piece of safety gear there is. Since you need one, I strongly advise getting the highest rating there is, a Type I. All Type I, II, and III vests are designed to keep the wearer afloat with his face out of the water. Type I PFDs do this best. If you are rowing a recreational shell, a PFD can be lashed or taped to the deck aft of the cockpit. If you are carrying your gear in kayaking bags, you can slip the PFD between the bag and its lashings. Don't store the PFD inside the bag. If you need it, you'll want to be able to get at it quickly and easily. Many racers are now using small PFDs that are inflated by CO_2 cartridges (not Coast Guard–approved at this writing). They are compact for storage, but very expensive. At least one has gone off accidentally, snapping the foot stretchers off the boat on which it was carried.

A shock cord running through small, permanently fixed guides holds a personal flotation device (PFD) in place. Attached to the life preserver are a battery-powered strobe and a whistle.

If you are rowing a traditional design, storage is no problem, but the location frequently is. Since it isn't used regularly, the PFD frequently finds its way to the bottom of the boat, under water bottles, anchor rodes, gear bags, you name it. Find a convenient, easy-to-reach place for your life preserver and *keep it there*. A friend of mine who rows a fixed-thwart dory ties his PFD under the seat, using very light line that he can easily break with his hands. It's out of the way and always handy. Aboard *Kavienga,* the PFD is held under shock cords on the stern flotation compartment. There it is easy to get at and keeps me from piling too much gear in the stern. It is a good idea to tie a whistle to your PFD. A whistle will help searchers locate you, because its sound will carry farther than your voice. A small hand-held strobe or flashlight attached to the PFD will serve the same purpose at night.

Aboard medium- to large-size power and sailing boats, Float Coats have become very popular. These are parka-style coats with built-in flotation. They are great on big boats, but I am not convinced of their value for rowing boats. They are thick, cumbersome, and long, and don't store well. If you already have one, or somebody gives you one as a gift, make sure you can row in it before you take it along—they are too expensive to be thrown out.

Survival suits have become big business with the offshore yacht-racing community. These are a great idea, but also bulky, heavy, and prohibitively expensive. Before a cruise some years ago, I gave some thought to what it would be like to be in the water, hoping to be rescued. The outcome of these reflections was a simple, homemade survival suit. I don't pretend it will take the place of the commercially available suits, but it's better than a pair of shorts and T-shirt and I feel better having it aboard. My survival suit is really just a full wet suit with some minor additions. The suit itself consists of Farmer John-style pants and a long-sleeved jacket, booties, gloves, and a hood. The Farmer Johns provide two layers of neoprene over the trunk of the body for added warmth; the booties, gloves, and hood keep the extremities warm. The additions were neoprene pockets, sewn and glued to the legs. The pockets, which close with flaps and Velcro, contain a whistle, a waterproof flashlight, two dye markers, and a strobe. The suit folds neatly and lives under the PFD aft.

If something happens and you end up in the water, *stay with your boat.* Anyone who has done any search-and-rescue work will tell you that a boat, even a small one, is far easier to find than a person. Staying with your boat will not only make you easier to find, it will probably also provide some extra flotation and may even allow you to stay partially out of the water. If you can pull up just the top half of your body on an overturned hull, you'll be better off than you would be in the water.

The greatest danger rowers face is being run down by larger vessels, and just about every other boat or ship out there is a larger vessel. Being narrow and low in the water, rowing boats are hard to see. Even small swells can easily obscure a rower. If he is in the path of the moon or the sun, the rower doesn't have enough mass to show up against the light. Even if the larger boat is using radar, it probably won't detect a rowing boat: fiberglass and wood are both notoriously poor reflectors of radar waves. It requires an alert person on watch to spot us, and many boats and ships do not keep a good watch.

If there were a choice, I would rather have to deal with large commercial vessels than pleasure boats. This may sound a little strange—I'll grant you that if you're playing tag with a freighter or tanker and he tags you, you'll lose in a big way—but I have my reasons. Long ago, I realized that if a collision between a rower and another vessel was to be avoided, the rower would have to be the one doing the avoiding. You can't count on being seen by the operator of any other vessel. If the rare one does see you, he probably doesn't understand the effect his wake will have on your boat. I prefer to dodge the big commercial craft simply because you can see them from farther off and get out of their way sooner.

From sea level, or 3 or 4 feet above it (eye height in a recreational boat), the oarsman's vision is severely limited. It is even more limited if there is a heavy ground swell running. The upper works of a freighter or tanker, or its running lights, can be seen from several miles away. Watch the approaching ship long enough to get an idea of where she is going, and head somewhere else. As you row, keep an eye on her in case she alters course. Whatever you do, don't try to race her. If she is cutting across your course, don't try to beat her unless you *know without a doubt* that the way is clear and safe and that it is better to go forward than backward. If there is *any* question in your mind, don't try it. Take a break, maybe eat a snack, and watch her go by. Don't think because she missed you, you are home free. Remember the wake. At speed, some commercial ships can kick up a wake that any surfer would love to ride. Be sure you have given yourself plenty of room and be ready to take the wave bow or stern on, whichever is best for your boat.

After commercial ships, my favorite boats for avoiding are sailboats. They're nice because their tall masts give you plenty of warning and they are usually slow. Being a sailor myself, I would like to believe the average sailor is keeping a better watch than his powerboating cousin, but I have evidence to the contrary. The trick to avoiding sailboats is in understanding their tacking and jibing angles. I once heard a rower complain that, no matter what he did, "this damned sailboat kept zigzagging and heading right at me." The boat was simply short-tacking out of the harbor. You must be aware of a sailboat's limitations and take these into consideration when avoiding them.

Large powerboats have the benefit of visibility, though they are frequently moving at such speeds as to nullify this advantage if you are trying to avoid them. As far as powerboats are concerned, the smaller they are, the worse they are. My idea of hell is to be made to row forever through a pack of small aluminum powerboats driven by overweight men wearing camouflage jackets, swilling beer, and trailing fishing lines. Small powerboats ride low in the water. Frequently the only way you know they're near you is by the sound of their motors. If there is a ground swell running, you will have to wait until you are up on a crest to look around for them, and pray they're not hidden from you in a trough. Since your hearing is your best defense against small powerboats, I strongly recommend that you not wear stereo headphones while you row.

There is some gear you can carry aboard that *may* make you more visible to other boaters for the purpose of avoiding collision or facilitating rescue. My friend who rows the dory with the PFD under the thwart has built a 6-foot mast out of a 1¹/₂-inch dowel. He fixes a small radar reflector to the masthead and lashes the mast forward. I have my doubts about its effectiveness, but it seems to make him feel better. You can also fix battery-powered running lights or "shake-and-break" chemical light sticks to your boat, but I wouldn't count on their being spotted. Go ahead and use anything you think will help, but keep a good strong flashlight handy so that you can shine it at the helmsman of an approaching vessel.

There is a wide variety of emergency gear on the market. Any good marine hardware store will have a section devoted to safety equipment, with strobes, whistles, flares, smoke bombs, air horns, flashlights, and more. Find out what your boat is required to carry by law and consider that gear to be the bare minimum. When you add to the required safety equipment, make sure you cover your bases, both day and night, by sound and sight. Make sure that the safety equipment you buy is Coast Guard–

approved, and check it regularly to see that it is in good working order.

Remember, if you are rowing after sunset, you have to be able to show a bright light, which normally means a flashlight. There are some great waterproof flashlights available today. I just bought a pair of Tekna lights, which are small and light and throw a powerful beam. I got two because I decided it seemed simpler than carrying spare batteries and a spare bulb. Besides, if I drop the light overboard, the spare batteries and bulb won't do me much good.

Bailers are vital to both your comfort and your safety. In earlier chapters, we discussed modifying your boat with a suction-style bailer or a bilge pump. If you're rowing a recreational shell and your suction bailer locks up, you can always bail with your cupped hands because your cockpit is very small. If you are rowing a traditional design and your pump breaks down, you will want to have at least one conventional bailer aboard as backup. Whatever you choose to use as a bailer, bucket or cut-down water jug, be sure you tie it securely to your boat. If you are swamped, you are going to want that bailer close at hand, not bobbing on the surface 15 feet away.

Filing a float plan is one of the best safety precautions you can take. Before you leave, tell someone—not just someone you meet at the harbor while you're getting ready to shove off, but a responsible person who cares whether you live or die—what your plans are. Provide as much information as you can: where you plan to go, possible stopping points along the way, a description of your boat, and anything else you can think of. Supply this person with the telephone number of the Coast Guard or Harbor Patrol. Then tell him or her when and how you will get in touch at the end of your cruise. If you don't make contact by the appointed time, your responsible person should notify the authorities that you are overdue. If possible, try to check in with him or her while you are on your cruise. The knowledge that you had passed the halfway point would reduce the search area if you didn't make contact at the end of the trip. Remember to make contact as soon as possible after landing. If you've asked someone to wait to hear from you, the least you can do is call promptly.

If your cruise or passage takes you far from shore, you might want to look into an emergency position-indicating radio beacon (EPIRB). When activated, an EPIRB automatically emits a radio beacon that a rescuer can home in on. The Class A EPIRB is stored in an inverted position and turns itself on automatically when turned upright. This works well on a larger boat, but it isn't practical aboard a rowing boat. A Class B EPIRB is turned on by hand and is probably the better choice for a small boat. Both the Class A and B units are designed for use more than 20 miles offshore, where their signals can be picked up by aircraft and military search-and-rescue facilities. The Class C EPIRB is intended for use closer to shore, as it uses the VHF/FM frequencies received by marine radiotelephones.

Two of the best pieces of safety equipment cannot be mandated by the Coast Guard or anyone else. These are experience and common sense. Experience comes only from time spent on the water, but common sense should not take so long to acquire. If you show up for a race and the wind is blowing 20 knots against a strong tide, with seas running six feet and building, you don't have to go out. If the conditions are worse than you've rowed in before, don't let the presence of other, more experienced rowers intimidate you. Ultimately, your safety is your own responsibility. You decide if you feel safe, you decide whether to go out or not. Don't let misplaced machismo or competitiveness put you in jeopardy.

The same holds true for the start of a cruise or long-distance passage. Just because you've made plans and told people what you're doing doesn't mean you have to go through with them if it isn't safe. You can always postpone your trip or make last-minute changes. If you do this, remember to let the person who has your float plan know about your new plans.

If you have begun your row and conditions deteriorate, don't be afraid to cut your trip short. When your trip stops being fun, when you have gear failure that you are unable to correct, or the weather becomes dangerous, stop! Your preparation and planning were designed to help you get out of such situations safely. If you have to cut your cruise or race short, don't consider it a failure, treat it as a learning experience.

Many people either row or started rowing for health reasons. If you have a health problem, see your physician before tackling an endurance row. Even if he was the one who originally suggested you take up rowing, a 100-mile cruise or 20-mile race may not be what he had in mind. Be sure to take any medication you need with you. Bring more than you need; your trip might last longer than you originally planned. Consider bringing twice as much as you need, dividing the amount between two bottles and storing them separately on the boat as a safeguard against loss or damage.

The same general considerations that affect your overall cruise planning will influence the provisions you make for first aid. An ounce of prevention, as always, is worth a pound of cure, but that doesn't excuse you from having to know how to handle emergencies. Don't assume that the first-aid kit you bought at the marine hardware store contains everything you need just because it has a red cross on it and is called a "nautical" kit. It might be perfect for your needs, especially if it has a good O-ring seal, but you should inspect the contents carefully and make changes as needed.

Take into account the nature of your cruising area and the length of your trip when you're filling your first-aid kit. If you're rowing the Connecticut coast from Stamford to Guilford to explore the Norwalk and Thimble islands, you probably won't need to pack much. It is a populated area with all the modern conveniences, and you will never be far from help. On the other hand, if you're cruising the Baja peninsula, you will be alone in a largely uninhabited area. You will need to carry quite a bit more, including a snake-bite kit.

The following list is not intended to cover all situations, but rather to provide a solid base on which to build.

First-aid manual	Aspirin (or equivalent)
Pepto-Bismol	Assorted Band-Aids
Sterile gauze pads	Sterile gauze roll
Adhesive tape	Finger and toe splints
Ace bandage	Antihistamine tablets
Eyedrops	Hydrocortisone cream

Waterproof sunscreen
Sudafed (or equivalent)
Scissors
Q-tips

Rubber bands
Polysporin (or equivalent)
Tweezers

Two items on this list are particularly important. The first is a high-quality, waterproof sunscreen. Even if you are already tan, you will need extra protection when you spend long days on the water. The second is rubber bands. If you slice a toe or finger badly, a rubber band makes an excellent tourniquet. Read about tourniquets in your first-aid manual before attempting to apply one. Consult your physician about any prescription drugs he thinks you might need.

If you're ready for a long-distance row, you've already faced the problem of seasickness and found what works best for you. If the over-the-counter medications haven't helped, ask your doctor for a prescription for Transderm Scop. Many people swear by these little Band-Aid-like patches, but be sure you try one or two before your long-distance row. A few people have bad reactions to them, and you don't want to find out you're one of them 15 miles offshore.

Cuts, burns, and blisters of varying degrees are the most common complaints on longer passages. *Read your first-aid manual before you go.* Learn to recognize the different types of burns and bleeding; know how to clean and protect a wound, how to use splints, how to find pressure points, and how to apply other treatments before you go. Taking a Red Cross first-aid course will stand you in good stead, even if you never injure yourself while rowing.

Heat can be extremely dangerous. Since you will be both doctor and patient, read your manual and memorize the *early symptoms* of heat cramps, heat exhaustion, and heatstroke, and their remedies. Ignoring these symptoms can prove fatal.

Cold can be just as deadly as heat. Extreme hypothermia can cause death, but even relatively mild hypothermia can cause a rower to become weak and lose his concentration. This can kill you as surely as severe cold. As with heat, prevention is your best defense. Read your first-aid manual on causes and treatment of hypothermia, and pay special attention to prevention. You must take care to keep warm and dry, because even mild water, especially in combination with a chilling wind, can lower your body temperature significantly. Know your rowing area, know the temperature of the water, and plan your clothing ahead of time. If there is the least chance you'll be cold, take good warm clothes and include a layer of waterproof gear.

If you go overboard, get out of the water as quickly as possible, and, unless the boat is in danger, concentrate on yourself. Hypothermia is best treated by warming the body *slowly,* to avoid overstimulating the pumping of cold blood from extremities to vital organs. Exercise, such as rowing, can overstimulate the flow of blood, as can hot drinks, caffeine, and alcohol. If you can get to shore without any problems, do so. If not, you will have to take care of yourself in the boat. Strip off your wet clothes, and lie down in a sleeping bag or wrap yourself in a warm blanket. If you can't do either, bundle up in the warmest, driest clothes you have. If you have to row, take it very easy. If you're rowing sliding-seat, use your legs as braces only and cut down the arc of your stroke.

If you are with someone else who is suffering from hypothermia, heat damp towels to body temperature and place them on the pulse points. Give warm nonalcoholic and noncaffeine drinks. Again, an ounce of prevention is worth a pound of cure.

Fatigue can cause real problems, but it is easily relieved if you are aware of it. With all the last-minute preparations for your trip, it may be difficult to start rested. Get a good night's sleep before you shove off—it will carry you a long way. Realistic daily goals will help reduce fatigue, as will eating well and getting plenty of sleep. If your trip is scheduled for a week or more and you begin to feel fatigue, think about cutting back on your daily goals. Spend more time on the beach or at anchor, and get more rest.

The foregoing is not intended to frighten the prospective long-distance rower, but rather to caution him. You will be entering an uncertain environment, and you must be able to take care of yourself. With the proper planning and forethought, your trip should be a safe one. I'm a real klutz around the house: I stub my toes on doorways, chairs, and table legs; I trip over the dog; if I go out to the garage to work with tools, the chances are good that I'll come back with a bloody finger. However, I have never suffered a major accident while rowing. Rowing is a safe sport, if you take the time to anticipate problems and exercise common sense. When I had a boat with an Oarmaster unit, I kept cutting myself on the sharp rolled edges of the tracks and stretchers, so I taped them over with duct tape. In many cases, safety is a matter of attending to the little things.

Chapter Nine

Sailing Rigs for Rowing Boats

A sailing rig is a natural complement to many rowing boats. Their easily driven hulls respond well to a minimal spread of sail, especially off the wind. Most traditional rowing boats were designed to carry sailing rigs; those that weren't can often be modified to do so. Books such as John Gardner's two-volume *Building Classic Small Craft* and his *Dory Book,* Willits Ansel's *The Whaleboat,* and John Leather's *Sail and Oar* include photographs, drawings, and plans for pulling boats with a profusion of sailing rigs. There is probably no way to propel a small boat by canvas that has not been tried.

If you are considering a sailing rig for your boat, ask yourself: Do you want a sailable rowing boat or two boats, sailing and rowing, in one? If you choose the former, you can use the sailing rig for auxiliary power, lightening your workload and expanding your cruising ground. The latter choice gives you a more efficient but also more complex rig, one requiring that the rest of the boat accommodate it to a degree not necessary for an auxiliary rig. You sacrifice a considerable amount of space with any rig when it is not in use, but if you want just an auxiliary, you can get away with a small amount of gear, just spars and sail. Depending upon the lateral resistance your hull offers, you may be able to sail only a few degrees either side of dead downwind without a rudder and leeboards, centerboard, or daggerboard, but if you plan your row properly, this should be fine. If a westerly fills in every afternoon on your regular rowing ground, start early and row due west. When you get tired, stop and have lunch, then turn around and hoist the sail. If your navigation and the expected westerly are both true, you should have a bracing sail back home, steering by the sheet. This is how I used *Kavienga's* sailing rig after discarding her leeboard and rudder. If, on the other hand, you want a true sailing boat, you will need to look into a rig that can sail to weather, and for this you will need foils.

A word of caution: Adding a sailing rig, even a small auxiliary sail, to your boat may change the way the authorities in your state view it. In most states, a boat powered solely by oars does not have to be registered and, therefore, taxed. As soon as you add a sailing rig, no matter what percentage of the time you use it, most states will treat your boat as a sailboat. Depending upon the boat's length and the laws of your state, this may mean you have to register and pay tax on the boat. It may also mean you have to install certain minimum safety gear, such as running lights. Be sure you want to deal with this before you decide to carry a sailing rig.

In Chapter 3, I described how *Kavienga* was designed to carry a sailing rig and how the rig eventually fell into disuse. This should not be misconstrued to mean that I dislike sailing. I love sailing, I just don't love sailing in a rowing boat. *Kavienga's* rig was discarded because of my minimalist tendencies. I rarely used it, so why carry it? John Garber made essentially the same decision after his cruise aboard *Gypsy Girl. Pogy,* his new boat, was designed and built as a rowing boat "to make life simpler." Yet conditions and preferences can always change. *Kavienga's* rig is carefully stored and could be brought back into use at any time.

When a boat comes with an optional sailing rig, don't assume the designer or builder gave the rig a lot of thought. Some sailing rigs are tacked on as an added incentive to the buyer without much thought being given to their efficiency or practicality. Some boats are designed so that they can only be rigged ashore. You will have to decide if such an arrangement suits you. Some require centerboard or daggerboard trunks, which in turn require rubber or plastic lips to keep the water out when the board is not in use. These lips can wear as the boat is dragged ashore. The trunks also add weight to the boat. If you don't care about windward ability and simply want to sail on a broad reach or downwind, you don't need a centerboard, daggerboard, or leeboard. Don't be afraid to modify a sailing rig, but on the other hand, before you add or change sails, think it over carefully. It would be a shame to cobble up a good rowing boat in an attempt to make a sailer out of her.

Take into account the size and type of rig, where and how it will attach to the boat, how it will be controlled and stored, and whether or not it will require hydrodynamic foils (rudder, leeboard, centerboard, or daggerboard), and, if it does, how these will attach to the boat. Look at boats similar to yours to get ideas.

There are almost as many different types of rigs as there are boats. If you desire a dual-purpose boat, one that can sail as well as she can row, talk to a sailmaker and the boatbuilder to learn what rig and foils they recommend and how to balance the rig against the foils. Depending on how much lateral resistance your hull offers, it may be possible to bring her up to a beam reach without using foils. If you are looking for an auxiliary, your task will be quite a bit easier. In the rest of this short chapter, we will review some of the auxiliary rigs available and look at a few of their strengths and weaknesses.

When selecting and building an auxiliary sailing rig for a rowing boat, the practical aspects of storage, stepping and unstepping the mast, and rigging and derigging the sail take precedence over pure sailing performance. Don't just think about rigging your boat at the beach or on a calm day; think about reefing the sail or unstepping the mast at sea in 18 knots of wind and 3- to 4-foot chop. You will need short, lightweight spars that are easy to store, set, and strike. You won't need a lot of sail area, but you will want a shape that is efficient off the wind, with a low center of effort to keep heeling to a minimum. Other, more modern high-aspect-ratio sail plans will work, but your center of balance may be uncomfortably high and your boat dangerously unstable.

You will want to be careful when deciding on sail area. I think it's natural to want the greatest amount of power possible. Most of our cars have horsepower to spare, but be careful with your sailing rig. In some cases, rigs in small boats can't be reefed quickly or efficiently, so it is wise to think of the sail area that will be appropriate for the strongest winds you expect to sail in. You will be a little slower when the wind is lighter, but that is safer than having to let the sheet run and pull down your rig if the wind becomes too strong.

To my way of thinking, *Kavienga*'s spritsail rig (see photograph, page 47) satisfied all these requirements. In most cases, the sprit rig is the one I would recommend to rowers who want an auxiliary. *Kavienga*'s rotating D-shaped mast is just 9 feet, and the sprit, $9^1/2$ feet. The sail is lashed to the mast and can be wrapped around both spars and secured with the mainsheet for easy storage. There are no battens to break or store, and the complete rig weighs in at just 6 pounds. The spritsail can be "scandalized" (that is, made to offer a smaller surface to the wind in a fashion quicker and easier but cruder than reefing) by removing the sprit, which can be done while sitting on the deck rather than standing in rough conditions. This results in a marconi rig with a very sloppy luff, but it is a safe way to shorten sail and produces a relatively efficient sail with a low center of effort. Without a boom to home in on your skull, the rig is easy to jibe.

The 55-square-foot vertical-cut sail is very efficient for broad-reaching and running, conditions that *Kavienga* enjoys, and offers just the right area for the normal afternoon breezes off Southern California. With 15 knots of wind over the stern or stern quarter, *Kavienga* is an exciting sailing boat. If it gusts over 18 knots, the rig can be taken down and she becomes an exciting rowing boat. Originally, the rig was sheeted with a double purchase line leading from the clew to a Harken block on a traveler, which consisted of a line dead-ended on both gunwales. When I stopped trying to go to weather, I discarded the traveler and the double purchase sheet, leading the sheet straight to my hand. Minimalism.

The gunter rig is frequently used on small boats for one of the same reasons as a spritsail: the spars are short and easy to stow. The gunter rig, an evolution of the standing lug rig, requires three spars: a boom, a mast, and a gaff, or yard, which is hoisted so that it extends almost vertically past the masthead. Set, the sail looks very much like the marconi rig and usually goes to weather

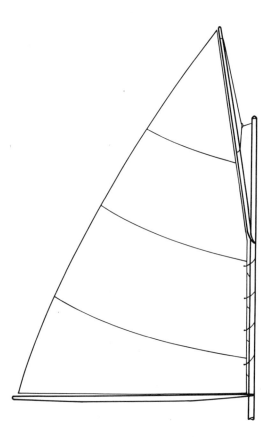

Gunter rig

quite well. In many small rowing boats, the boom could get in the way. The same sail area in a spritsail would provide a lower center of effort and therefore less heeling. Of course, the spritsail will not go to weather as well as the gunter. There are various ways to reef the gunter rig. If this is the rig you choose, each should be examined thoroughly before you settle on one.

The lugsail is a very old quadrilateral sail design, the head of which is secured to a yard. Most of us know the variation of the lugsail called the Chinese lug from pictures of junks. There are also the dipping lug, the balanced lug, and the standing lug. Apart from having been used for centuries in the Orient, these sails gave their name to fishing boats called luggers and are still commonly used today on small craft.

Lugsails are great for small boats because they set a large amount of sail low down on short, easily stored spars. Their low aspect ratio keeps heeling to a minimum, while their relatively large sail area provides plenty of power. If you are making your own spars, an easy matter with this simple rig, be sure the yard is light and stiff to make hoisting easier and prevent sag. You might investigate the use of composites in the yard to make it as light and stiff as possible. In most small-boat applications, lug rigs will be unstayed, relying on the mast step and mast partner along with the mast's inherent stiffness to keep them up.

Let's take a brief look at the variety of lugsail rigs available, though you will find a book in Suggestions for Further Reading that can give you far more information.

The Chinese lugsail, also known as the junk rig, is a wonderful design that has been used successfully in the Orient for hundreds of years and has even achieved some popularity in the smaller classes of singlehanded transatlantic racing yachts such as Blondie Hasler's (later Michael Richey's) folkboat *Jester*. Like other lugsails, it sets with the luff forward of the mast, giving a clean airflow. The Chinese lug's greatest advantage and, to my mind, what makes it the least attractive of all the lugsails for a rowing boat is its full-length battens. They hold the shape of the sail and allow the camber to be adjusted by means of sheets leading from the trailing edges of the battens (one sheet for each pair of battens) to the mainsheet block and then aft. Reefing is easy: simply drop a batten down on the boom and make it fast. I know there are those out there who swear by the junk rig, but I just can't live with all the gear. Boom, yard, full-length battens, and extra sheets are just too much for me on a rowing boat.

The foot of the balanced lug is attached, usually laced, to a boom, which, like the yard, extends forward of the mast, placing the luff of the sail in undisturbed air. It is an efficient, low-aspect-ratio sail, but I don't see the need for carrying an extra spar when it isn't necessary.

Boomless rigs are the way to go in rowing boats, and to that end you might want to investigate two variations on the lugsail theme. The dipping lugsail is tacked to either a hook or snap shackle forward. When it comes time to tack or jibe, the tack is

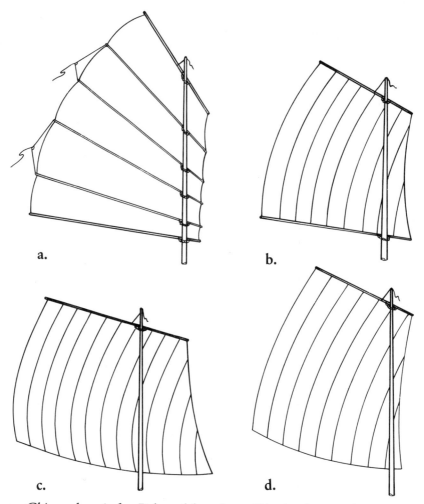

a. *Chinese lug rig* **b.** *Balanced lug rig* **c.** *Dipping lug rig* **d.** *Standing lug rig*

unfastened, the halyard eased, and the sail is lowered until the yard can be easily reached. The halyard is unfastened; the sail and boom are passed around the trailing edge of the mast; the tack is reattached to the hook or snap shackle; and then the halyard is reattached and the yard rehoisted to leeward. That is quite a bit of work. Granted, if you are using the sail to get home on a predictable wind, you might never have to change tacks. But you can't count on it.

The fourth lugsail variation, the standing lug, is in my opinion the best lugsail for the present purposes. It is simplicity itself: a mast, yard, halyard, and sheet. A standing lug rig of a given size will be slightly heavier than the spritsail rig due to the fact that the yard must be more rigid than the sprit, and it has one more piece of line, the halyard, but it too is a very light rig. In rough conditions, the sail can be reefed, lowering its center of effort and reducing its area, and the halyard can be led to the weather rail to act as a shroud, though in boats as narrow as most traditional designs, this may offer little advantage. The tack of the standing lugsail is tacked down permanently, either to the mast or the deck. On this rig, the yard is permanently set on one side of the mast, so the tack has been brought aft to limit the amount of sail area with disturbed airflow when the yard is to weather. If you have rigged the boat to carry the yard on either side of the mast, know your course and the prevailing winds. You can set up the boat so the yard will be to leeward most of the time.

If you like to tinker with your boat and experiment with new things, here are some sources of possible inspiration for you. I once saw a dory with a sailboard rig stuck in its mast partner. The wishbone booms were gone and a sheet was tied to the clew. I have no idea how effective the rig was: the long mast and battens might have made it difficult to store aboard, but the owner of the dory seemed to be enjoying himself, and that's what it's all about.

If you have access to old copies of *WoodenBoat* Magazine, look up number 48, September/October 1982. On pages 52–55 are some very interesting photographs and drawings of sails that Douglas Martin experimented with when he was building his experimental rowing-sailing boat, *Mockingull*. Some of his ideas might apply to your boat or spark some ideas of your own. See also *100 Small Boat Rigs,* by Philip Bolger. This book is full of rig ideas—some elegantly simple, some outlandish. It doesn't offer the detail you need to build a rig, but it's a great place to start.

Roger Taylor of Camden, Maine, suggests what he calls "motor sailing," that is, using sail and oars simultaneously. I must confess I've never tried it, since all the boats I have had with sailing rigs have been too tender. I have had to sit to weather to balance the force of the rig. "Motor sailing" sounds like great fun, though, especially when sailing dead downwind in light airs.

I now pass along to you an idea that I have been mulling over for years, but have somehow never found the time to explore fully. It might be the ultimate minimalist sailing rig for a pulling boat. I once saw a small picture in a magazine showing a rather beamy sliding-seat rowing boat sailing dead downwind, propelled by a small spinnaker set on a vertical scull. A sock or sleeve had been sewn to the head of the spinnaker, and this slipped over the blade of the scull. I don't remember seeing a downhaul, but a simple Velcro closure on the narrow neck below the blade would serve. With very broad shoulders, the small spinnaker was obviously cut for dead downwind work. As I remember the photograph, sheet and guy were led to a man sitting in the center of the boat, allowing him to trim the sail and steer with the lines. The foot of the chute might open better if you led the lines through the oarlocks, forcing the sheeting angle to be wider, and sat in the stern. If it worked (and why shouldn't it?), it would be the ultimate "sailing home package." The tiny chute, with sheets, would weigh under 1 pound and could be stored in a very small pouch. A word of caution: If I were going to use a scull for a mast, I would make sure I was carrying a spare.

The possibilities for rigging a sail are almost limitless. I encourage you to explore some of them.

Chapter Ten

Two Cruises

This chapter tells the story of two cruises, taken in different parts of the world in different types of boats. These two journeys serve to illustrate the diverse experiences available to the cruising oarsman. They also reveal the similarities in planning and preparations involved in such undertakings. While both of these cruises were made in sliding-seat boats, this in no way implies that fixed-thwart cruisers are inappropriate or passé. Fixed-thwart cruising has one main advantage over sliding-seat: it conserves energy. A fixed-thwart oarsman can brace his feet or fold one under the thwart as John Garber does, and row with a nice, steady, energy-conserving stroke. He will be slower than the sliding-seat rower, who burns up a tremendous number of calories, but he can go a long way without feeling tired.

I had not made a cruise aboard *Kavienga* for almost two years. I had made modifications to my 16-foot peapod (see Chapter 3) and I had rowed her regularly, but no long distances had been attempted. Something told me it was time to start planning more than a daily row. Since I already had the boat, all I needed to do was to figure out when to make my cruise and where to go. Early spring seemed a good time to take off, for no other reason than I was starting to plan in February and it would take a month or two to get ready.

For some time, three destinations had been vying for attention in the back of my mind. Every day, I would see the bulk of

Catalina Island on the horizon and daydream about circumnavigating the 19-mile-long island. The most popular offshore destination in Southern California, Catalina is crowded in summer but virtually deserted at other times of the year. Its rugged, untouched landscape reminds one of what California must have looked like before freeways and housing developments. My thoughts about Catalina got as far as a simple plan. I allotted five or six days for my trip, expecting to row most of the time in the lee of the island or with the normal westerlies at my back. In the end, the Catalina trip was postponed. The weather would be better in late September or early October. April still sees the occasional front bringing wind and rain from the northwest.

The second destination I had been toying with was Lake Powell, on the Arizona-Utah border. Lake Powell was created when the Colorado River was dammed at Page, Arizona. Before Glen Canyon Dam, the area was a mini-Grand Canyon. Now it's a Grand Canyon with a floor of water. As with Catalina, the Powell trip was postponed when I discovered the weather was not ideal in early April. A friend who had taken his powerboat to the lake the year before told me the nights could be freezing. Besides, he too wanted to row the lake, but couldn't get away until early June. We decided to make the trip together, and I contemplated my third destination.

A Baja California Cruise

To many in the West and Southwest, Baja California is a handy playground. Windsurfers, dirt-bike riders, surfers, four-wheel-drive fanatics, and others regularly flock to the rugged, unspoiled desert and its pristine shores. For some time, I had entertained the idea of a cruise on the Sea of Cortez. My ultimate goal was to explore some of the Midriff Islands, near the center of the 800-mile-long sea. Before going that far afield, I thought it best to try out the northern end of the sea, where conditions were similar to those I would find farther south.

I had been to Baja several times and knew some people who had rowed there, but I felt the need to do more research. There is a good selection of books on Baja and the Sea of Cortez. For several weeks I read, planned, read some more, and changed my plans. Lists of needed equipment kept growing, but *Kavienga*'s capacity did not increase accordingly. The more I read, the more I felt I was taking my life in my hands venturing into Baja. Each book stressed the lack of facilities and the desolateness of the area. In retrospect, I see that the books weren't exaggerating the remoteness of the area, but neither were they presenting a truly balanced picture. One book mentioned the possibility of bandits.

I had spent enough time in Baja to know that the guidebooks were portraying Baja in such a way as to make people think twice, but that they were accurate in advising visitors to bring everything they might need. There are no convenience stores on the coast of the Sea of Cortez. As items were checked off my lists, the garage began to bulge with gear. I repeatedly went through the pile, evaluating each piece of equipment a second and third time, discarding some items but adding others. In a final weight-saving move, the anchor chain was taken out of my ground tackle, and my tent was set aside. I copied appropriate pages from the Baja guidebooks and talked to friends who had rowed in the same area, making careful note of what they told me. Mexico may be right next door, but it is a foreign country. Along with all the gear and provisions for the trip, car insurance, a Mexican fishing license, and a tourist card had to be obtained.

While reading and planning, I trained, spending more and more time in the boat each week. I felt strong enough for the trip, but needed to put in time just sitting in the boat, getting my body used to the hours aboard. I rowed five or six days a week, four or five 5- to 6-milers and one 15-miler. As my departure date neared, I carried a pair of sandbags in the boat to simulate the weight of my provisions.

Planning and anticipating a cruise can be challenging and fun, but eventually you have to move from theory to practice and actually get in the boat. San Felipe, my launching point, is a long way from Southern California. I left for Mexico the day before the planned start of my row. *Kavienga* and three sculls were securely tied on top of my truck; the bed was full of provisions and gear. Four hours of driving got me to the border crossing at

Mexicali, where I picked up Mexico Highway 5, a two-lane road through the desert that terminates 130 miles later in San Felipe.

In town, I bought fresh shrimp at the harbor and some wonderful local sweet rolls called pan dulce, corn tortillas, and a jar of salsa at a general store on a sandy side street. Then I drove back up Highway 5 and turned off on a rough dirt track leading to a rugged campsite on the coast just above town. For a fee, the caretaker said he would watch my truck for me, and I had no choice but to trust him.

The afternoon was spent transferring gear from the truck to the boat and carefully storing it. Then I took a bearing on Punta Estrella, the only major point of land between me and my first day's destination, did my reciprocals, and made a note of the first course I would row. Once everything was set, I made a small fire with wood purchased from the caretaker and barbecued the shrimp. Night fell while I was enjoying my shrimp and salsa and reviewing my plans for the cruise. If I had attempted to use my borrowed Coleman stove that night I would have discovered a problem that was to plague me for the entire trip. And even if I had discovered it, I don't know what could have been done about it.

The schedule for the cruise was quite open. Having allotted six days, I was carrying provisions for seven. These could be stretched if the need arose. I gave my wife a float plan and told her to expect to hear from me in eight days. The rough strategy was to head south, hugging the coastline, for three days, then turn around and come back. If I made it as far as the tiny fishing village of Puertecitos, 51 miles down the coast, that would be fine. If I didn't, that was fine too. If anything caught my interest, I would stop and explore for as long as I wanted. The goal of the trip was to get away and become familiar with the desolate coastline in preparation for a more ambitious cruise later, not necessarily to reach a predetermined destination. I put out my fire and turned in early—the next day was going to be a busy one.

On the Sea of Cortez, a rower's schedule is dictated by the tides. Spring tides can range up to 20 feet in height, and they are tricky. Parts of the sea can be in ebb while other areas are experiencing a flood. The University of Arizona produces a tide table for the area, but careful observation is still very important.

My goal for the first day was ambitious. I wanted to spend the night at Bahia de Santa Maria, a bay 20 miles south of San Felipe. The plan was to leave camp just before high water on the assumption that it would be better to row against the tide early, when I was fresh, than at the end of the day. Bahia de Santa Maria is a large, shallow bay that empties at low tide, putting the beach on which I intended to camp a mile from the water. I hoped to arrive at the entrance to the bay just as the tide was turning and ride it to shore.

Kavienga seemed almost hopelessly loaded down as I pushed her off the beach just before sunrise. The heaviest single provision was water. The Baja coast is not beach as most of us know it, it is desert, and I wanted to be prepared. Eleven half-gallon plastic water jugs, 44 pounds of water, were scattered around *Kavienga*. To these were added seven pint containers of grapefruit juice. I was allotting myself 3½ quarts of liquid per day and did not feel overprepared. In my first-aid kit were some Halizone tablets to treat any questionable water I might pick up en route. Along with 51 pounds of liquid was the mountain of food and gear I had lugged down with me, all carefully stored in Bone Dry bags. *Kavienga* sat low in the water. I breakfasted on a large pan dulce with Australian tinned butter and a pint of grapefruit juice, thereby lightening my load by just over a pound. After a few stretches, I climbed aboard and slid out the Concept IIs. *Kavienga* moves best when rowed at a relatively low stroke rate. At 18 spm she felt sluggish, but this was no race. If I didn't make Bahia de Santa Maria, it didn't really matter, I had chosen an alternative camping spot.

A few shafts of light were spearing the sky over the eastern horizon as I passed Punta de Machoro at the north end of San Felipe. Moments later, the whole eastern sky turned a bright reddish gold and a beam of light found Cerro el Machoro, the 940-foot peak of Punta de Machoro. Three miles later, with the swollen reddish orange ball of the sun hanging above the horizon, I passed Punta San Felipe, where the ice plant is located. By this time, *Kavienga* was over two miles offshore, heading out to round Punta Estrella south of the town. She felt less sluggish, and it seemed that landmarks on shore were passing faster. The tide had evidently turned and was giving me some assistance. I passed the harbor, where shrimpers rafted up and pangas were dragged ashore, then the hotels at the south end of town.

It may have just been the exuberance of the first day's row, or the extra push of the ebbing tide, but *Kavienga* cleared Punta Estrella well ahead of schedule and I set my course for Bahia de Santa Maria. Some gulls checked out *Kavienga,* but when it was apparent that there was no bait for them, they departed. A huge flock of brown pelicans, flying single file, glided past silently, their long wingtip feathers nearly brushing the surface of the water. Terns dove for small fish. Except for the birds, *Kavienga* could have been alone on the sea.

A light northwesterly came up and combined with the ebbing tide to give me a little extra push, making 18 spm feel like a very easy pace. I knew I would make my landfall at Bahia de Santa Maria. *Kavienga* actually reached the entrance of the bay too soon. The tide was still ebbing when I got there. A white-brown line of breaking water, caused by the tide boiling over the bar at the bay entrance, greeted *Kavienga.* A single bright sail cruised slowly off the mouth of the bay, a boardsailor also looking for a way back to shore. A mile away, on the clean white sand of our goal, I could see a half-dozen bright sails and two vehicles beside a pair of tents.

The windsurfer sailed over, dropped his rig, and sat on his board while we discussed our dilemma. He was from San Diego and it turned out we had some common acquaintances. He and his friends had been camping on the beach for three days, suffering through a wind drought. When the northwesterly came in at high water that morning, he had gone for a sail. The wind remained light and he didn't get back before the tide was almost out. He guessed that the bay was less than a foot deep, too shallow for his daggerboard, so he planned to beach his board at the southern entrance to the bay and walk to camp. He told me that the bar at the entrance was soft sand and mud, probably 8 inches deep. I decided to try it, rather than camp at the entrance. The foot of water inside was enough, and I only had to row a mile against the current to get where I wanted to be.

While the windsurfer sailed to a beach below the wide entrance to the bay, I looked for low spots in the wall of frothing water, theorizing it would mark a deeper channel. I shifted a few water bottles and my kayaking bags to the very stern, trimming *Kavienga* in a bow-up mode, and drove for a promising spot on the bar. For a moment, it was like rowing through a washing machine as *Kavienga,* even heavily laden, bounced around like a cork. Then the peapod was across the bar into flat water.

Once inside the bay, I had the feeling I was rowing at 8 or 9 knots as the water sped by, but I wasn't putting much distance between myself and the bar. The speed was an illusion caused by the fast ebbing tide. I was getting pretty tired, without making any significant progress, when my starboard oar scraped bottom. My low stern dragged for an instant and I knew there was no way I was going to make shore before running out of water. It was more important that I stop the tide from washing me back across the bar. I pulled in the oars, grabbed the anchor, and tossed it as far ahead of me as I could. While *Kavienga* rode the tide back toward the Sea of Cortez, I hastily shortened up on the rode and made it fast. The anchor skipped along the bottom for a few yards, then caught and held. I sat panting as the tide rushed out of the bay. After rewarding myself with a long drink from a water bottle, I watched the retreating water and some dark shapes racing for the sea. Rays—the shallow bay would be full of them at high tide, something to remember if I went wading.

Half an hour after crossing over the bar, *Kavienga* was high and dry on the sandy bottom of Bahia de Santa Maria. I had almost made it; I was only a mile short of my destination. My first thought was to unload some of my gear and carry it to the beach. Then I remembered I was in Mexico, the land of *mañana*. The tide would come back, and in three or four hours I would be able to row to shore with it. I adjusted my broad-brimmed straw hat and looked around.

The boardsailor I had met earlier was walking toward me from where he had landed, and six other figures were approaching from the beach. I had not expected a welcoming committee. We introduced ourselves and fanned out, exploring the bottom of the bay, discussing their wind safari and my rowing adventure as we picked up sand dollars and other shells. A small ray trapped in a pool was given a wide berth. By the time we reached their camp, we were all hot and tired. They had two vehicles, a Chevy van, which was stuck up to its hubs in the soft sand, and a 4x4 Toyota pickup. A large awning was rigged off the van, and we all sat and rested in the shade. The windsurfers seemed to think that rowing was a strange sport, but I countered, saying it was no stranger than negotiating 20 miles of nearly impassable dirt road to sit on the edge of the desert and wait for wind, which didn't appear to be cooperating.

One of the sailors kept checking the condition of the water at the bar through a pair of binoculars and finally announced the tide was coming in. They invited me to camp with them and I accepted, then started the long walk to where *Kavienga* waited patiently for me and the water.

I miscalculated the time it would take to walk out to the boat. With no idea how fast the tide would flood into the bay, I took my time, pausing to look for shells. I was just halfway to *Kavienga* when I realized the water had already reached her. Since her anchor was securely dug in, I wasn't worried that she would float away, but I didn't want to swim to her or wade through ray-infested water. I started to jog. When I reached the water, or the water reached me, I broke into a run. The water quickly rose to my calves and forced me into a slow, shuffling walk, clearing any rays from my path. By the time I reached the boat, the water was waist deep and she was bobbing happily. I climbed aboard and rowed to the beach.

The northwesterly had filled in to a pleasant 12 to 15 knots, providing some relief from the heat. The boardsailors hit the bay while I laid out some of my gear and relaxed in the shade of their awning. One of the books I had read while planning the cruise was the Automobile Club's guide to Baja California. The guidebook had described Bahia de Santa Maria as a "rustic campsite." If *rustic* means there is nothing there, then the guidebook hit the nail right on the head. There were some unoccupied round brick houses with thatched roofs, evidently owned or leased by Americans, and that was it. The boardsailors had even brought their own firewood. One thing they hadn't brought was a radio or tape player, instinctively sensing that any loud music would have been out of place in that primordial land.

That night, I discovered the problem with the stove. A week before leaving on the trip, I had started to clean my own stove and found it was broken. I borrowed a nice Coleman stove from a friend and assumed I was all set, but this stove was also broken. At first, it wouldn't pressurize; when I finally got it going, it went out almost immediately.

The boardsailors shared their campfire with me while they told horror stories of the dirt road down from San Felipe and tried to decide if they would pull out the following day. While we ate and talked, everyone took a shot at fixing the borrowed stove. After two hours and several applications of Crazy Glue and duct tape, the stove was declared fixed.

We had finished dinner and I was thinking about heading back to my sleeping bag, when we heard the unmistakable sound of a rattlesnake. I had never heard one in the wild, but there was no doubt in my mind as to what it was. We all scattered as fast as we could. While the boardsailors went back, armed with sticks and flashlights, I cautiously lifted my sleeping bag into *Kavienga*. After convincing myself a rattler couldn't slither over *Kavienga*'s sleek glass sides, I finally fell asleep.

I awoke before dawn, debating what to do on my second day. Bahia de Santa Maria was interesting and I wanted to explore, but if *Kavienga* missed the morning high water, I would have to wait to leave until late afternoon, when it was hotter. I had no special goal for my second day, though I had penciled a tiny question mark at Punta San Fermin, 20 miles farther south.

I had no idea what I'd find at Punta San Fermin except that Arroyo Matomi meets the sea at that point. Covering 20 miles would mean that Puertecitos would be an easy row the following day. As the sun exploded out of the eastern horizon and the tide flooded the bay, I loaded *Kavienga* and watched a great blue heron stalking the shallows. By the time the sun was up, *Kavienga* was loaded and ready to go. Two of the boardsailors were awake and I shared the last of my pan dulce with them and had a cup of tea heated on their camping stove. The "repaired" Coleman eluded testing. Just as I was about to go, I discovered that the previous afternoon's northwesterly had left a layer of grit on *Kavienga*. I took the time to clean the seat tracks and oarlocks, then shoved off.

The second day's row was peaceful. I passed two small camps where 4x4s were parked and saw another boardsailor, but I didn't speak to a soul. After three hours in the boat, I touched shore at a wide sandy beach that looked as though it had never seen a human. I stretched my legs, had a light lunch sitting on the sand rather than on *Kavienga*'s sliding seat, slathered my body with sunscreen, and watched pelicans, gulls, and terns work over a school of small fish just offshore.

The activity in the water reminded me of the fishing pole stowed aboard. I quickly assembled my short pole and spinning reel and tied a feathered jig to the line. I am a passive, rather than an active, fisherman. My idea of fishing is to troll the lure, and if it happens to pass a fish and the fish chooses to bite, then I will try to reel it in. I pushed off, put out what I thought was an appropriate amount of line, and took up the oars. I hadn't taken 10 strokes when the line sang off the reel. I dropped the oars, set the hook, and tightened down on the drag. Less than 5 minutes later, a nice bonito was splashing alongside *Kavienga*. I passed a line through its gills to tow it aft and cast out again. The oars were still trailing when the line once again began to sing out. Five minutes later two bonitos bobbed in *Kavienga*'s wake and the rod was stowed. I had more than enough fish for dinner.

Kavienga was moving easily, but I was hot and tired. I'd had it for the day and was ready to find a spot to camp. With the oars pulled in, I was half-twisted around in the seat, looking for Punta San Fermin, when *Kavienga* gave a terrible lurch. I slid the oars out for stability and looked around to see what had caused it. *Kavienga* was alone on the sea, a mile and a half from shore. A swirl of water aft caught my eye and I watched as a black scimitar pierced the surface. Through the sun-dappled water, I saw the body of a shark. Its tail flicked almost lazily as it drove for *Kavienga*'s stern. The boat twisted and bobbed as I realized that the shark, about a 5-foot blue, was eating my dinner. I grabbed the trailing line and yanked the bonito aboard. The line came easily, bringing the head of one fish and about two-thirds of the other. The shark made another slow pass and rolled over on its side, looking up at me with one large, unblinking eye. I had the disturbing feeling I was being warned.

After the incident with the shark, I headed *Kavienga* toward shore. I rowed in stern first, looking for landmarks on the featureless shore. Punta San Fermin was still down the coast. As on the day before, I was about a mile short of my goal. It didn't matter, the beach was clean and untouched, with some magnificent cholla cactus as a backdrop. The tide was out and the high-water mark was about a quarter of a mile inland from where I had beached, but I was getting used to that.

My dining plans had changed twice that day. Originally, the plan was to have a can of beef stew, then it changed to fillet of bonito. Now, thanks to the shark, I was back to beef stew, but there was enough bonito left to make an appetizer of seviche. I cut up the fish, put it in a shallow pan, then squeezed in the juice of two limes, added a chopped tomato, some diced onion, and half a diced green chili. I didn't have any cilantro, but I was camping and figured I had to rough it. While my appetizer marinated in the shade of the dodger, I went exploring, keeping a careful eye on the incoming tide. Later, when the tide lifted *Kavienga,* I rowed to the new shore and set up camp. That night, I learned that my stove was not really fixed. The only way it would maintain a flame was if I constantly pumped gas by hand.

There is a small bay just north of Puertecitos where some native pangas were moored well out, near the entrance. I reached it early in the morning of the third day. *Kavienga* had just passed this bay, her course set due south for the point protecting Puertecitos, when I heard the roar of an outboard. A Boston Whaler's blunt bow appeared from among the pangas I had just passed. Two Americans in their early teens were aboard. Waving and shouting, they did a high-speed doughnut around *Kavienga,* then applied full power and headed south. I was left rocking viciously in their wake and thinking unkind thoughts.

I reached Puertecitos well before noon. The small town wraps around a shallow bay that faces southeast. The tide was still high enough to allow me to row almost all the way to shore before grounding on the sand and pebble bottom. The Boston Whaler used by my welcoming committee was tied near the rough concrete launching ramp on the eastern side of the bay. My guidebook described Puertecitos as "an unpolished resort." Looking around, I felt the book was being unnecessarily generous. It seemed that much of the town was made up of trailers and ramshackle bungalows, vacation homes for Americans. There was a restaurant on the beach in front of me and, as I knew from the guidebook, an airstrip behind it. The book had also revealed the existence of some natural hot springs on the eastern point, out past the launching ramp. I had reached my goal and was disappointed. The most interesting place on the trip had been Bahia de Santa Maria.

With *Kavienga* on the ground, I took a few minutes to organize the boat and take inventory. There was a general store in the small town that would offer the opportunity to stock up if anything was low. There was still food for four and a half days, though I seemed to have been drinking my water and juice a little faster than planned. Consuming the water had the advantage of making *Kavienga* lighter, but I decided to add another gallon, the improvement in my safety more than offsetting the extra weight.

By the time inventory was finished, the bay around me had dried out and I became aware of the high-pitched whine of motors. Adjusting my wide-brimmed straw hat to block the sun, I saw three Quad Runners approaching across the shoal. The four-wheeled motorcycles carried Americans in their middle teens, each with a beer-can holder bolted to the handlebars and one with a huge tape player strapped on the luggage rack. I could hear their music over the collective noise of the three motors. They split into two groups, passing on either side of *Kavienga* and kicking up a wake of wet sand and pebbles. They made my decision for me: I would shove off as soon as the tide would permit.

I didn't like leaving *Kavienga* unattended and kept my eye on her while walking the half-mile up to the shore. I found the store; quickly bought a gallon jug of water, a cold can of orange juice, a jar of salsa, and some fresh flour tortillas; and hurried back to *Kavienga,* drinking the juice as I went. My peapod had attracted a small knot of young Mexicans, all standing at a respectful distance. My Spanish is practically nonexistent, but I smiled and they smiled. They watched while I stored my gear. Then an older man with the weathered face of a fisherman arrived to shoo them away. He spoke quite a bit of English, and we chatted briefly about my boat and his town.

The sliding-seat rowing rig fascinated him, as did the carbon fiber sculls. I told him about enjoying Bahia de Santa Maria. He smiled and told me a long story about sailing on a shrimper out of San Felipe when he was younger and being stranded at Santa Maria for two weeks with a broken engine. He too had enjoyed the bay's peacefulness.

The three young Americans on their Quad Runners stormed by us, their motors and music interrupting conversation, and my new friend suggested his town was more pleasant to visit during the week. I had lost track of time and forgotten it was Saturday. Since he had been eyeing my five empty plastic water jugs, I asked my friend if he had any use for them. He did, the fishermen used them as floats. I gave them to him, gaining some space in the boat. His way of thanking me, it turned out, greatly exceeded the value of my gift. Finally, he told me he had to go to work in the restaurant and ambled away.

I was trying to decide which of my canned delicacies would be the least offensive cold, as I had no desire to wrestle with the stove to prepare lunch, when a small boy ran across the shoal toward me. He stopped running about 10 yards away and approached shyly, offering me a paper bag. I smiled at him and accepted the offering, and he was off like a shot. The bag contained a ripe avocado, a tomato, and a foil-wrapped bundle. I peeled away the foil to find a half-dozen large shrimp, sautéed to perfection, and two soft flour tortillas. I waved in the direction of the restaurant, though I was too far away to be seen, and quickly made two huge shrimp tacos. The trip to Puertecitos had been worth it after all.

I didn't make it to Punta San Fermin that afternoon, but camped at the base of an unnamed arroyo 5 or 6 miles north of Puertecitos. Just before beaching, I landed another bonito. After battling the stove, I dined on fish tacos, not as good as lunch, but far better than something from a can.

With high tide around 0930, I decided to rise early, row a few hours, then beach the boat while the tide ebbed, and maybe row again after it turned. My internal clock woke me at 0400. I wanted a cup of tea, but not enough to face the recalcitrant stove. After a pint of juice, I struck camp and was on the water by 0430. Another brilliant sunrise silhouetted two shrimpers working sev-

eral miles offshore, and not long after I caught a long, lean barracuda on my trolling jig.

By 0930, I had reached an area of "rustic campsites" where
there were four or five trucks parked on the beach. I rowed on for
several miles, fighting the ebbing tide, because I still felt fresh and
didn't want to beach right at high water. Finally, I rowed to shore
between two camps and anchored *Kavienga* in shallow water a
quarter of a mile offshore. When the tide left her aground, I
cleaned the barracuda, struggled with the stove, and once again
made fish tacos. Tacos for three meals out of the last four was a
bit much, but it used up the tortillas, tomato, and salsa (the
avocado had gone with the shrimp). The beach offered very little
of interest, so I rearranged *Kavienga* to permit a nap with my head
in the shade of the dodger.

The incoming tide woke me, and by the time *Kavienga* was
afloat, I was ready to press on. I entertained no hope of making
Bahia de Santa Maria that afternoon, but another 10 miles of
rowing would put the bay within easy striking distance the following morning.

That night I came in on a deserted beach somewhere south of
Bahia de Santa Maria. I hadn't been there 15 minutes when a tired
old jeep with no muffler arrived. What caught my attention was
the shotgun in a leather scabbard on the driver's side. Remembering the warnings about bandits, I smiled broadly. The driver, a
Mexican in his early twenties wearing cowboy boots, faded
jeans, a purple Western shirt, and a red baseball cap, told me I
owed him $2 for using his "camp." I paid and settled down to
fight the stove and make dinner.

The tide was still flooding and the sun was well up when
Kavienga pulled into Bahia de Santa Maria on the fifth day. I had
the feeling I was coming home. It was Monday morning, there
were no vehicles on the beach and no sign of people around the
brick houses. Seeing the bay full of water, I realized there was a
small island, really only a high sand dune, near where I'd camped
before. I steered *Kavienga* toward it, figuring it should be free of
snakes.

It was a delightful little islet. It reminded me of a whale's
back. At high water, the white sand mound was about 40 feet

long, 20 feet wide, and, at its highest point, 3 feet above the water. I felt it deserved a name, and I named it Moby Island for its shape and color. I buried *Kavienga*'s anchor in the dry sand, then pushed her back out so that the tide would reach her well before high water.

The tide quickly ebbed, leaving *Kavienga* aground 70 feet from the high-water line on Moby Island. I carried some of my gear ashore, then went exploring. If you avoided looking at the round brick houses, it was easy to imagine no human had ever set foot at Bahia de Santa Maria. I walked out to the sea and watched terns diving on small fish, then returned slowly to Moby Island, now just a hill surrounded by drying mud and sand.

Kavienga had taken on a certain odor over the past few days, an odor that intensified as the sun climbed in the sky and the heat increased. She was beginning to smell like dead fish. The bonito and barracuda had left their scent behind. While the tide was out, I transferred all my gear and the rowing rig to Moby Island and, when the tide came in, used my bucket to wash her down. While pumping her dry, I realized that this was the first time on the trip I had used the new bilge pump. After sponging her out and restowing all the gear and provisions, she smelled better and was ready to go. There was plenty of food and water left, so I decided to extend my cruise and spend another day at Bahia de Santa Maria. This would give me time to do some exploring, and, besides, I was sore from spending so much time in the boat.

In the late afternoon, a 20-knot northwesterly blew in across the desert, bringing sand and grit with it. At sunset it subsided. I cleaned the oarlocks and seat tracks of the dirt, then battled the stove to make a simple dinner. It was pleasant waking up the next morning and not having to jump into the boat and row. I stayed in my sleeping bag and read, then made a light, cold breakfast and followed the ebbing tide out to the sea, picking up seashells as I went.

By the time the tide started to flood in late afternoon, I had decided that if I stayed any longer I might never leave. I loaded up *Kavienga,* took in the anchor, and stepped aboard, waiting for the water. When she was finally afloat, I rowed against the tide to the entrance of the bay, drove across the fast water at the shallow bar and headed north, riding with the tide. San Felipe wasn't my goal, but I wanted to do 10 miles and camp somewhere between Punta Diggs and Punta Estrella so that there would only be 11 or 12 miles to row back to the truck the following morning.

That night I camped on a rocky beach in the shadow of Punta Estrella and ate a huge dinner. I was 3 hours' rowing time from my truck, and I rationalized that it would be easier to carry food in my stomach than in *Kavienga*. There was plenty of food left, the fish and shrimp having stretched my rations considerably. I was glad, however, for the extra gallon of water bought in Puertecitos. By extending my trip, I had used up everything I had brought with me.

Kavienga's hull ground onto the sand in front of my truck at 0800 on the seventh morning of the cruise. It had been a nearly perfect trip. I know some sailors who almost hope something will break on their boat so that they can show off their ingenuity by making repairs at sea. That is not my idea of fun. To me, a well-planned and well-executed cruise is one in which nothing goes terribly wrong. I get nearly as much pleasure from knowing I planned and prepared correctly as I do from the cruise itself. Everything had gone well, I had learned a lot and was looking forward to planning my cruise to the Midriff Islands.

A British Columbia Cruise

As the summer of 1986 drew to a close, Chris Maas and his partner Greg Shell began thinking about an adventure that would get them away from the shop and the day-to-day pressures of business. It dawned on them that no one, to the best of their knowledge, had ever made a cruise in an open-water rowing shell. The idea took hold and they were soon figuring out where they wanted to go and the logistics of carrying cruising gear aboard a pair of shells.

Their destination was easily decided. Maas already planned to take his Aero to Seattle for the Great Cross Sound Race. From Seattle, it is only a short hop across the Strait of Juan de Fuca to

British Columbia, Canada. Maas had lived in Canada for a while and "knew how pretty it is, and that a lot of the area is accessible only by boat." When he lived in British Columbia, he had tried sailing to some of the areas he now wanted to explore and knew that the wind rarely blew hard there, a good omen for a cruise in open-water rowing shells. Together, Maas and Shell looked at charts of the land north of Vancouver, known as "British Columbia's Sunshine Coast," and talked to some people who had cruised the area. Maas had always wanted to see Princess Louisa Inlet, and they talked to some cruisers who had made the journey. Stories of the rugged shore and beautiful waterfalls quickly convinced them that this was where they should go.

To reach Princess Louisa Inlet, they would have to row up twisting Jervis Inlet. Carved by glaciers, Jervis Inlet is more river or fjord than inlet. Hundreds of feet deep and only 1 to 1¹/₂ miles wide, Jervis Inlet meanders through some of British Columbia's most beautiful scenery. The inlet is divided into three "reaches": Prince of Wales, Princess Royal, and Queen's. They would launch from the Sechelt Peninsula, and their ultimate goal would be Chatterbox Falls at the base of Princess Louisa Inlet. Malibu Rapids, the entrance to Princess Louisa Inlet, was about 50 miles up the Jervis Inlet; the waterfall, another 5 miles. They obtained a Canadian chart and started planning in earnest. Maas says, "In the time we had, it looked like Princess Louisa might be too far." They wanted to see the country, not sprint to the inlet and back.

One of the people they talked to warned them that the coast would be very steep and that they might have trouble hauling out. Maas dismissed this information, figuring there is always a place where you can haul out a recreational shell. He was to learn differently.

Maas admits, "This was not a well and thoroughly planned expedition," but whether or not it was consciously planned, the combined experience of these two boatbuilding oarsmen guided their preparations in the proper direction. Their first priority was to determine how they would carry their gear. After some research, they bought four vinyl kayaking bags. When Maas races his Aero, he straps his PFD on the deck aft of the cockpit, so he and Shell decided to use the same method for lashing the kayak-

Greg Shell's Vancouver 21, rigged for cruising with kayak bags strapped fore and aft. (Photo courtesy Greg Shell)

ing bags to the boat. Maas's Aero already had four holes drilled in the hull-to-deck joint lip aft. They lashed one of the bags in place with shock cord, liked it, and duplicated the mounting on the foredeck. Shell's Vancouver presented a different challenge, since it was an older boat with a blind seam joining hull and deck. They solved the problem by pop-riveting four small pad eyes to both the fore and aft decks and lashing the bags to these.

Once the question of how to carry gear was answered, they had to figure out what gear to take with them. They arbitrarily decided that 30 pounds per boat would be about right. In Maas's words, they carried "pretty much what you would carry on a week-long hiking trip." Maas, an avid outdoorsman, already owned a North Face dome tent and a pair of goose-down sleeping bags by the same company. Maas says that if he had not already had the sleeping bags, he probably would have chosen synthetic ones, but his didn't get wet, so there was no problem. His stove, an MSR Firefly, is light, compact, and efficient.

Knowing there would be plenty of water along the way, they stocked up on freeze-dried food for the trip. When they started, they each carried a gallon of water aboard, but fresh water was so plentiful that they whittled this amount down to just one water bottle each. They also took a good supply of trail mix and candy bars.

Since Maas had lived in the area and knew they could expect pleasant weather, they chose to take minimal clothing. Maas and Shell decided against carrying much in the way of first-aid supplies or repair gear. Maas describes their first-aid kit as "pretty minimal" and says they took very little repair equipment because, "unless something weird happened, like one of the boats got thrown up on the beach, the boats would be under far less strain than when racing, and we wouldn't be gone long enough to wear anything out." The gear they carried consisted of "some tools, spare fins, and an extra oarlock and pin." They did not carry an extra oar.

After the cruise, Maas said, "As it turned out, we could have gotten by with a lot less. The weather was warm and calm and nothing broke. Equipment-wise we had plenty of stuff. My tendency is to carry too much stuff if I'm not sure of exactly what I'm getting into. All we could have used more of was candy and trail mix."

After the Great Cross Sound Race, in which Maas won his class, they drove to Vancouver to make final preparations for their trip. From Vancouver, they drove some 45 miles north to launch from an unnamed cove on the Sechelt Peninsula. By the time they had the gear divided so that all four bags weighed about the same and had the bags strapped on the boats, it was quite late. Before launching, they had not had the loaded bags aboard the boats, and Maas was surprised to find that the addition of 30 pounds did not affect his Aero's handling all that much. He reports that she was "slow to accelerate," but that she rowed well. Of course, the loaded weight of the Aero was 70 pounds, much less than the hull weight of some other recreational rowing boats. As soon as the boats were in the water, Shell and Maas discovered there was a 1-to-1½-knot current running out of Jervis Inlet.

Their first day's row was just 5 miles, across Skookumchuck Narrows and around Egmont Point, to a gravel beach on the eastern shore. Remembering the warning that they might not be able to find a beach, Maas had to agree that it wasn't easy. "The cliffs are pretty sheer and there really aren't that many places to stay." Their first beach was a narrow indentation, and they "slept right at the edge of the water." As would become their practice, they did not set up their tent that first night. Maas says, "There was never any need for it; it never rained, and there were no insects."

They set no daily distance goals; they simply looked on the chart to see what interested them and headed for it. With the steep, heavily wooded walls of the inlet only a mile and a half apart, even though both boats were equipped with compasses, they navigated by sight only. The second day, they left early in the morning, choosing Vancouver Bay on the eastern shore as their morning destination. Once again the current was against them, contrary to the indications of the tide table. On the 8-mile row, they were accompanied by seals. Although they saw an occasional fishing boat, there was no one on the desolate shore.

They arrived before noon, "scrounged up some oysters, and cooked them in their shells." Maas reports that as the cruise wore on, he "got pretty sick of oysters." It was warm and calm, so they had a long swim before climbing back into the boats and heading north to Glacial Creek. In the afternoon, the current was still against them. They decided it was caused by the runoff. So much water was pouring into the inlet that it overwhelmed the normal tidal pattern. Shell describes the steep landscape surrounding the inlet as "magnificent." He said they tended to forget they were rowing after a while and just enjoyed the passing scene.

Their second night was spent on the pebble beach at Glacial Creek. An abandoned logging camp on the eastern shore, Glacial Creek intrigued the two men. It was warm on the beach, but all around them the snow line was just at 4,000 feet. They fished with no luck. Shell reports that he took over the cooking chores from Maas. It seems Maas hadn't been measuring the water he added to the freeze-dried food. According to Shell, their food got quite a bit better after he started doing the cooking. That night, a seal surfaced near shore with a loud breath and both men nearly jumped out of their sleeping bags, convinced a grizzly had found their camp.

They left early the following morning with the hope of getting to Princess Louisa Inlet. Their goal was still 20 miles away. Maas says they reached Patrick Point on the western shore, about halfway to the entrance to Princess Louisa Inlet, and held a meeting. Patrick Point is the natural break between Princess Royal and Queen's reaches. If they went on, they would have faced a long row up Queen's Reach, another row through Malibu Rapids before entering Princess Louisa Inlet, then another long row to Chatterbox Falls at the head of the inlet. They decided that if they kept going, they would end up just having to turn around and row back. They rowed to shore, climbed out on a narrow rock ledge, leaving the boats tied to a tether in the water, and had lunch. Instead of going on, they decided to go back and explore Glacial Creek.

They hugged the western shore on the way back. For the first time, the current was with them. When they wanted to rest, they could just hold their oars out in the rest position, lie down in their boats, and watch the magnificent scenery glide past. Returning to their previous night's camping spot, Shell discovered a deep pool at the base of a waterfall. Both men said it was beautiful, but filled with snow melt, so they swam only briefly.

They stayed at Glacial Creek that night. The next morning, they hiked up an abandoned logging road to the snow line. Shell said that he was amazed at how the timber company had "raped the land," that he hadn't seen anything like it outside of a strip-mining operation. That afternoon they returned to the pool for another quick dip in the near-freezing water.

The following morning, they awoke to the first wind they encountered on the trip. A 20-knot breeze was blowing straight down the inlet. With the wind behind them and the outflow pushing them along, they made the 25-mile return to the Sechelt Peninsula in a single long day of rowing. Shell celebrated his thirtieth birthday rowing back down Prince of Wales Reach.

While Maas and Shell did not reach their destination, Princess Louisa Inlet, they did achieve their main goals. They enjoyed themselves and proved that recreational shells can be adapted for short cruises. Maas feels they could easily have stayed out twice as long as they did. The main advantage traditional designs have over recreational shells, where cruising is concerned, is their greater carrying capacity and the fact that you can sleep in them.

These two cruises took place in different types of boats and in different environments. Maas and Shell spent more time exploring the shore, while I spent the bulk of my time concentrating on making my ultimate destination. In both cases, the cruisers enjoyed themselves and learned some vital lessons about this extension of their sport.

Chapter Eleven

The Catalina to Marina Del Rey Rowing and Paddling Derby

Almost since its inception in 1977, the California Yacht Club's Catalina to Marina del Rey Rowing and Paddling Derby has been known as "the Catalina race" or, among competitive rowers, simply "Catalina." In the first 10 years of its existence, it became a major event in open-water boat design and the ultimate goal of long-distance rowers on the West Coast. The race started modestly enough. In 1977, a long-time oarsman and California Yacht Club member, Charles Hathaway, rowed across the 32-nautical-mile channel to mark his fiftieth birthday. The row became an annual event, its object being merely to finish.

It didn't take long for this event to develop into a race of major proportions, with its own history and traditions. Steve Hathaway, Charles's son, set a singles record rowing his Martin Trainer in the 1983 race. That record held until 1986, even though most of the top open-water oarsmen took a shot at it. *Millennium Falcon,* a three-man, high-performance, wooden dory equipped with Oarmasters, was designed and built specifically for the race. *Falcon* won the extremely rough 1981 event, came back as a quad in 1982 with four Oarmasters, and won again. Some intriguing triples from Santa Cruz and San Francisco have come south with mixed results. Gordie Nash's California Wherry, an old design brought back to life, found its niche in rowing history by winning its class in the 1984 race.

153

Through the years, the race has mirrored and influenced the dramatic changes in outlook and boat design in the sport. Karen Carlson, who made her third trip across the channel in 1986, credits the California Yacht Club with being the first to recognize women rowers by giving them their own class. The goal of the race is no longer to finish, it is to win and set new records. The boats are no longer tricked-out traditional designs or Aldens, they are state-of-the-art racers, developed specifically for open-water conditions.

Certain years have developed their own mystiques, adding to the appeal of the event. Nineteen eighty-one is remembered as a rough year when most of the competitors failed to finish. Nineteen eighty-five is remembered not only for the escalation of the design and building battle, which saw Nash's modified ARS vying against Hertig's super-trick Laser, but also for rough conditions and the tremendous contest in the triples class. Shirwin Smith and Hillary Dembroff recruited Dolly Stockman, an East Coast sculler with no open-water experience, and added her to the Small Craft Triple Nash had made for them. Their only competition that year was Craig Rogers, Bill Simpkins, and George Blackwell in another triple from central California. After nearly six hours, the women finished 4 seconds behind the men to cheers from the racing committee and spectators alike.

Gordie Nash first discovered the Catalina race in 1978 and has raced in it every year since. The race and the training it has required of him have taught Nash a lot about open-water rowing and influenced the boats he has modified and helped design. The Small Craft Double was a direct result of Nash's association with Small Craft and his win in the 1983 doubles class aboard a modified Alden Double. In Chapter 3, we saw how Nash modified a Small Craft ARS and turned a Small Craft Double into a triple for the 1985 event; and how Tad Springer of Laser took a giant step forward, converting a double into a lightweight single in which Per Hertig won the singles class. We also learned how Nash designed and built his own new-generation double for 1986 and recruited Kevin Strain as his rowing partner for the express purpose of smashing the existing doubles record.

Nash was not the only person working on a new boat or getting ready for the 1986 Catalina race. In a case of parallel

The seating arrangement in a Maas Dragonfly (29 feet 3 inches by 27 inches by 80 pounds). Note the compass for the bow man and the Stroke-coach for the stern, or stroke, seat.

evolution, Chris Maas was developing his own Dragonfly Double at the same time that Nash was working on the Pacific 30. These two designs represent the new generation of competition doubles, doubles that are faster than singles. This is not as strange as it sounds. Until the introduction of these two new 30-footers, recreational doubles were relatively slow boats. They had a lot of potential, but it was never fully tapped. First of all, doubles were too short. Before the Small Craft Double was introduced, they were at most 20 feet long and weighed well over 100 pounds. Builders seemed to be laboring under the illusion that boats had to be short for people to lug them around and heavily built to withstand the strains of two-man rowing. Short, in any boat, means slow; and *heavily* built and *strongly* built are not synonymous terms.

Doubles seemed to be an afterthought, put together by builders to meet the demand of a small segment of the market. The builders erroneously viewed this portion of the market as husband-and-wife duos, or parent-and-child teams, out for a leisurely row in quiet water, not as serious rowers interested in open-water racing or cruising. The Small Craft Double may have been the first step away from this design tendency, but if it was a step, the boats by Nash and Maas represent a giant leap. Both the Pacific 30 and the Dragonfly are long, lean, light, strong boats designed to be at home in open water.

One of Maas's Dragonflies was to be rowed by the women's team of Linda Locklin and Karen "KC" Carlson from Santa Cruz. Another Maas design, the Aero, was rowed by Mark Steffy, who directs the Tahoe Rowing Club, deals in Maas designs at his Rower's Boathouse, and organizes the North Tahoe Rowing Regatta. Before the start of the race, Maas and Steffy made some minor modifications to the sleek Aero, adding a small splash guard forward of the cockpit and inserting a large Dragonfly fin in the fin box to keep the boat tracking in a heavy cross sea. Steffy had already made some of his own additions to the boat, which are detailed in Chapter 3.

Bob Jarvis of Santa Cruz had recently acquired the prototype Robinson/Knecht and the rights to produce her. The design appears on the chart in Chapter 2 as a "stable racing shell." At 23 1/2 feet, the Robinson/Knecht (now known as the J-Shell) is not the longest recreational single around, but at 17 inches wide, she is by far the narrowest. Her 40-pound weight puts her on a par with the Aero and the Pacific 24. The Robinson/Knecht was originally designed as a trainer for scullers, but Jarvis added some internal stiffness, modified the cockpit to take an Elvstrom bailer, and won the five races he entered before the Catalina race.

The day before the race—the day that boats are loaded aboard their escorts and taken to the island—found Bob Jarvis working frantically in the California Yacht Club parking lot. Though he had driven thousands of miles with his boat on top of his car without problems, his special seat had blown out on the drive down from Santa Cruz. The original seat on the boat had 14-inch axles and was designed to ride just inside the splash box. The designers had done this in order to be able to shorten the seat deck, so that the rowers would not be banging their calves at the catch. The seat deck had been reduced to a tiny step for use while boarding the boat. Replacing the seat on short notice was impossible, because there just aren't that many seats with 14-inch axles around. Therefore, Jarvis had to buy tracks and a standard seat and build a new seat deck out of plywood. He finished in time and loaded the boat onto his escort for the long trip to the island.

The stage was set. Gordie Nash and Kevin Strain had trained for a year and practiced visualizing themselves setting a new record. All they needed to do was go out and do it. Mark Steffy and Bob Jarvis were set to do battle in boats they both believed in. Karen Carlson and Linda Locklin had only one competitor this year—the clock. There were 18 other competitors, all eager for the race. At harbors up and down the Southern California coast, competitors loaded their boats aboard escort vessels and started for Catalina's Isthmus Cove.

Early October may well be the ideal time to visit Catalina Island. The weather is good, and most of the tourists have gone back to the mainland. The escort boats made the long passage over the glassy seas and took moorings in Isthmus and Fourth of July coves. As soon as the mooring wands were picked up, many of the competitors put their boats in the water for a brief afternoon row while their supporters listened attentively to marine weather forecasts.

The early morning clouds and fog that sometimes blot out the Southern California sun for a week at a time in early summer are long gone by October. The winter storms are still four or five months away, but the Santa Ana winds, the hot dry winds that whip off the inland deserts at up to 50 knots, are a seasonal threat. The air had a certain "Santa Ana feel" to it, warm and dry, and everyone waited anxiously for the weather report.

While Gordie Nash secluded himself, listening to quiet music in preparation for the next day's race, most of the competitors, the owners and crews of the escort vessels, and the organizers

Gordie Nash and Kevin Strain load their Pacific 30 (30 feet by 29 inches by 85 pounds) for the trip to Catalina.

enjoyed a huge dinner ashore. The weather forecast was not good: possible Santa Anas were predicted for the following day. Chuck Wright, the event chairman, quietly circulated among the competitors, polling them about an earlier start, in an attempt to avoid the strong headwinds. The traditional early-morning starting time had been moved up so that competitors could cross the shipping lanes in daylight. The later start was a welcome change, but if the Santa Anas developed during the morning, the racers might find themselves rowing into strong headwinds as they neared shore. The organizers decided to stick with the planned starting time, which turned out to be a good thing.

Soon after everyone was asleep, the Santa Anas whipped across the channel and battered the island. With the winds ricocheting off the island's sheer rock cliffs, it was hard to judge their true strength, but the escort fleet rocked and rolled in the normally placid waters. More than one competitor got up to make sure his rowing boat was safely lashed to the deck. By the time

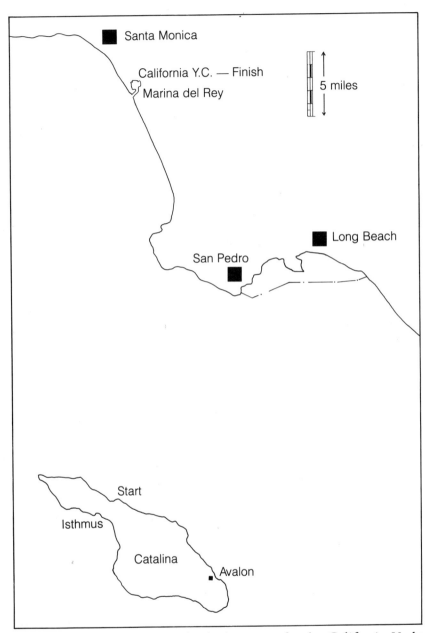

Catalina Island and the mainland, the venue for the California Yacht Club's Catalina to Marina del Rey race.

people began to launch, the winds were gone and the sea was flattening. Competitors breathed a collective sigh of relief as they taped hands, slipped on gloves, and readied their boats for the ordeal to come.

Gordie Nash and Kevin Strain were among the first to launch, one hour before their scheduled start. Boats started individually, in reverse order of their potential speed. The boats the organizers thought would be the slowest went off first. Gordie Nash and Kevin Strain would start last. While their competitors started off into the darkness with their escorts in their wakes, Nash and Strain warmed up. According to Nash, "In our minds we knew what we wanted to do, we had trained all summer, we had a new boat, all the equipment, we knew exactly how fast the boat could go and how fast we could go. We knew in our minds we could do it, we visualized going across the finish line in 4½ hours. Now we just had to show everybody else that we could do it."

Game plans, which had been meticulously developed on the trip over, took some time being put into operation. Most of the rowers had not met their escort skippers until the day before, and navigation problems, which had seemed so simple in the daylight, now had to be worked out in the darkness. Many rowers couldn't see their compasses in the dark, so the responsibility for navigating shifted to the escorts. Rowers who had thought the escorts would simply be following them, had to learn how to read navigation lights and place themselves directly in front of their escorts, adjusting their course to match that of the larger boat. Communications occasionally broke down during this trial-and-error phase.

Bob Jarvis may have suffered the most from a communication breakdown. Navigation responsibility belonged to his escort vessel, *Andrea*. After Jarvis started, *Andrea* had to maneuver through some heavy traffic around the line, and Jarvis, watching her running lights, thought she was trying to indicate to him he should alter his course. Due to a bend in the California coastline and the way Catalina Island lies, the course from the Isthmus to Marina del Rey is almost due north. Jarvis headed off strongly in a northeasterly direction, outdistancing his escort.

For the first hour, Gordie Nash and Kevin Strain rowed at over 8 knots. With the exception of Bob Jarvis, who appeared headed for Long Beach, Gordie Nash and Kevin Strain were on the most easterly course. Next came Mark Steffy, then Carlson and Locklin, with the rest of the fleet spread out to the northwest. After the race, when Nash was asked about their seemingly low course, he laughed and said; "We were right on rhumb line. There's a secret to crossing that channel. After nine years I've learned it, and I'm not telling what it is!"

At sunrise a school of dolphins surged through the fleet, briefly pacing some of the rowing boats. Jarvis realized the entire fleet was well north of him and swung through almost 90 degrees to head up to them. Mark Steffy, rowing his first long-distance ocean race, had started at a near sprint and was flagging. His wife, who was also his trainer, says, "Mark was poorly paced for this race." Steffy hung on, got his second wind, and continued toward Marina del Rey.

Bob Jarvis overcorrected and wound up high of the course, just above Carlson and Locklin in their double. He finally regained his escort boat and got back on course. Suddenly he was in the water. One of his foot stretchers had pulled loose, and he pitched out of his boat. Jarvis spent 20 minutes in the water, trying to fix his boat while *Andrea* hovered nearby. Finally, he climbed back aboard and once again took up the oars. The stretcher broke again and he was doomed to finish the race using only one leg to drive his stroke.

The water stayed mercifully smooth and the winds remained light as the fleet converged on the Marina del Rey entrance. The radio net announced, "Gordie and Kevin are approaching the breakwater, Gordie's screaming for grapefruit juice, we can't tell if he's delirious or not." The California Yacht Club's manager, Tony Dix, aboard Mark Steffy's escort, *Owen Churchill,* immediately radioed the club office to have the bar send down an ample supply of juice for the man who was knocking a great chunk of time off the record.

Gordie Nash and Kevin Strain crossed the line off the Yacht Club dock in an elapsed time of 4:37:23, taking 43 minutes off the old record. Margie Cate and Craig Leeds, rowing one of Nash's

Pacific 30s, set a mixed doubles record at 5:10:51. Rowing against the clock, Karen Carlson and Linda Locklin brought their Maas Dragonfly in at 5:28:26, setting a new women's double record. In spite of all his problems, Bob Jarvis still managed to set a new singles record when he finished after 5:27:02 on the water, beating Mark Steffy by 23 minutes. A combination of ideal conditions, a year of rigorous training, and design and building improvements produced records in five out of the six rowing classes. The 1986 Catalina to Marina del Rey Rowing and Paddling Derby not only went into the record books, it rewrote them.

All those who played a significant role in the 1986 Catalina to Marina del Rey race returned in 1987. As Nash put it, "I live for this race. I plan my year around it." Some other competitors might not be quite as hard-core, but everyone who showed up at the California Yacht Club for the eleventh running of the event had put in many months of training and preparation.

One might have thought Nash and Strain's record-shattering 1986 performance would scare away competition in the men's doubles class, but it seemed to have the opposite effect. Six other teams showed up to row against the Pacific 30. The most interesting of the challengers was probably the father-son team of Steve and Charles Hathaway. Both men hold records in the singles class, but it was the first time they had combined their skills and experience to do the race in a double. After the 1986 race they ordered a Pacific 30 from Nash, then spent the summer racing in some of the tough Central California races. Also entered were two teams from Santa Cruz: Gus Ballas and Neal Snyderman in a Maas Dragonfly, and Bill Simpkins and Craig Rogers in a Pacific 30. The always tough team of Jim Flack and Scott Ellsworth made the long haul down from San Francisco with their well-campaigned Maas Dragonfly. In preparation for Catalina, they had won both the Lake Tahoe North Shore event and the Sausalito Open Ocean Regatta. No one expected to see Nash and Strain's 1986 record broken, and several knowledgeable observers opined that to break their time of 4:37:23 would require a new design, but there were boats and rowers on the water to keep them honest.

Shirwin and Marie seconds after setting a record in the women's doubles class.

Bob Jarvis was back, this time with one of his production J-Shells. After his navigational and gear problems of the previous year he knew his own record was "soft" and was intent on bettering it. His competition promised to be better, too. A second J-Shell was entered, with Walter Edberg from Los Gatos at the sculls, and there were three Maas Aeros, a Maas Vancouver 21, a Pacific 24, and a 24-foot Laser double rigged as a single. Everyone knew there would be no slack in the singles class; anyone rowing a poor course or suffering a gear failure could not hope to win in a class with that depth.

Margie Cate and Craig Leeds were back with a Pacific 30 to defend their 1986 mixed doubles record against the Sausalito team of Kate Erhart and Mark Kelly in a Maas Dragonfly. The class that many were expecting to provide the closest racing was the women's doubles. Karen "KC" Carlson and Linda Locklin returned with their Maas Dragonfly, but this time they would not be rowing just against the clock. Shirwin Smith had planned to enter in her Maas Dragonfly with her regular rowing partner, Hillary Dembroff. Early in the season the two ladies had won their class at Tahoe, but Hillary had subsequently injured her back. Shirwin recruited Marie Hagelstein, who regularly dominates the women's singles class in a Maas Aero, as her new partner. Before joining Shirwin in the double, Marie's impressive 1987 record included class wins at Tahoe, the Sausalito Open Ocean Regatta, and the San Diego Bay to Bay Race, giving her a virtual lock on the annual class trophy. Injury continued to plague Shirwin's team; two days before Catalina, Marie injured a finger when she jammed it into the side of a pool while swimming. Undaunted, she bent the finger to fit an oar grip and taped it in place. A third women's double was entered for C'Anne Cook-Steffy of Tahoe Rowing Club and her partner, Vera Strock, both new to the Channel crossing. Their double was also a Maas Dragonfly, pitting the three ladies' teams against each other in equally matched boats.

Significantly, of the 20 rowing boats entered, 19 represented the modern open-water design and building methods of the Central California boatbuilders. Eleven entrants came from the design board and shop of Chris Maas: seven Dragonfly doubles, three Aeros, and a Vancouver 21. Nash's Pacific line was next, represented by five Pacific 30 doubles and a Pacific 24. Bob Jarvis's brace of J-Shells made up the balance of the 19. Designed and built independently, these boats all share common traits and show the direction open-water rowing is taking. They are light, stiff, and strong, designed to be rowed competitively and safely in open water. They have hard decks and small, sealed cockpits. The sole exception among the 1987 entries was a Laser double rigged as a single—similar to the boat Per Hertig rowed in 1985. In terms of boat design and construction, 1985 seemed like a light year ago.

With the strongest fleet in the history of the regatta and a hurricane off Baja California threatening to spin wind and rain into Southern California, chairman Chuck Wright wisely compressed the starting sequence, sending boats off at two-minute intervals. First to start, at 0500, was Skip Lind in his Laser. Last away were Nash and Strain.

Nash and Strain winning their class.

The 1987 trip across the Channel was rougher than the year before, but not dangerously so. Margie Cate and Craig Leeds led the boats across the finish line—20 minutes ahead of Erhart and Kelly—winning their class and beating their own 1986 record time. Bob Jarvis once again won the singles class. Rowing a straighter course than the previous year and suffering no break-downs, he bested second-place finisher William Berger by over 20 minutes and beat his own record. In the women's doubles, Shirwin and Marie smoked across the channel, beating KC and Linda by about 15 minutes and breaking the Santa Cruz pair's year-old record in the process. The only class not to set a new record was the men's doubles. Predictably, Nash and Strain again won the race, ahead of Gus Ballas and Neal Snyderman, who had a tight race with Bill Simpkins and Craig Rogers for second. In the hard-fought class, Flack and Ellsworth finished fourth, only minutes ahead of Charles and Steve Hathaway.

After long hot showers and a bit of rest, the luncheon got underway. Trophies, participation plaques, and T-shirts were handed out, and the owners of the escort vessels, without whom this great classic race could not be held, were all thanked. Then Chuck Wright made a special presentation. In honor of his tenth trip across the Channel, Gordie Nash was made an honorary member of the California Yacht Club; the plaque that Wright gave him not only commemorated his ten races, but also honored him for his commitment and contributions to the sport. Deeply affected, Nash accepted his award to a thunderous standing ovation from those who know him and appreciate what he has done for open-water rowing.

Appendix

How to Find Your Way
in the Rowing Underground

There is no central, complete source of information about rowing. In the absence of a central clearinghouse, a sort of rower's underground has developed, and the developing rower will benefit from tapping into it. Things are better now than they once were. There used to be no publications covering open-water rowing, and word of mouth was the only way rowers learned about other rowers or boatbuilders. I remember trying to track down a boat in the middle 1960s. I had heard stories of a wooden dory being rowed in Newport Beach, 14 miles from my home. In the market for a new boat, I spent a lot of time searching for the dory. It seemed several people had seen it, but nobody knew who owned or had built it. My questions led me to two backyard boatbuilders I didn't know existed, a group of three rowers who thought they were the only ones in the area, and finally to the man who had sold a pair of oarlocks to the dory's owner. In that way I located the builder. As it turned out, I didn't like the boat, but the search was interesting. I bought a boat from one of the two boatbuilders it led me to and rowed many miles with the trio of rowers I met. That rowing underground is still in place, and it is still the best source of information about our sport.

Communication is a problem. People are frequently confused and misled; they don't know where to take lessons, how many boats are available, or where to find them. Those who own boats and want to race or cruise in company have trouble learning about events. There are some publications that can help, and they are listed here, but many large publications are dated; businesses start up and fold or move, and clubs always seem to be in a state of flux. The best advice I can give is to find an event, go to it, and talk to other rowers. In this way you can begin to develop a network of friends who row. Most rowers will know other rowers, and I have yet to meet one who didn't like to talk about his sport. Through this network and the publications you can keep in touch with what is going on.

American Rowing, the organ of the United States Rowing Association, 251 Illinois St., Suite 980, Indianapolis, IN 46204, is published bimonthly. Their focus is still somewhat narrow, centered on flatwater rowing, but they are beginning to pay more attention to open-water rowing. Their calendar lists many open-water events.

California Open Water Rowing Association, Yacht *Fairhaven,* Foot of Spring St., Sausalito, CA 94965 publishes a monthly newsletter with brief articles on rowing events. It contains an extensive calendar of races, cruises, gatherings, and seminars, which makes it worth its weight in gold.

Messing About in Boats, 29 Burley St., Wenham, MA is published twice monthly with articles on rowing and small-boat cruising.

Small Boat Journal is published bimonthly by SB Journal, Inc., P.O. Box 400, Rt. 9 West, Bennington, VT 05201. *SBJ* frequently reviews rowing boats and gear and has an annual issue with a large rowing section. Their calendar also regularly lists open-water rowing events.

In addition, some boatbuilders, rowing shops, and clubs publish newsletters that can offer a wealth of information.

The following is a list of addresses of companies mentioned in this book, or other places where you can get information on boats and rowing.

General Shell Corp., Yacht *Fairhaven,* Foot of Spring St., Sausalito, CA 94965. Builders of copies of traditional boats (both fixed thwart and sliding seat), clearinghouse for information on used boats and some hardware.

Maas Boat Co., 1453 Harbour Way South, Richmond, CA 94804. Builders of the Aero, Vancouver 21, and Dragonfly; also a source for some hardware.

Pacific Rowing Crafters, 247 Gate 5 Rd., Sausalito, CA 94965. Builders of the Pacific 18, 24, and 30, and a source for some hardware.

R.J. Jarvis Co., 114 Parkway South, Santa Cruz, CA 95062. Builders of the J-Shell and a source for some hardware.

Small Craft, Inc., P.O. Box 766, Baltic, CT 06630. Builders of Warning, Lightning, ARS, Typhoon, and Small Craft Double, and a source for some hardware.

Open Water Rowing, Foot of Spring St., Sausalito, CA 94965. A school specializing in open-water rowing; also offers open-water shell rentals, sales, and storage, along with clothing and some hardware.

The Santa Cruz Rowing School, P.O. Box 7782, Santa Cruz, CA 95062. A school specializing in ocean rowing.

Boathouse Row Sports, Ltd., 2501 Olive St., Philadelphia, PA 19130. Offers clothing and some hardware and acts as an unofficial clearinghouse for names and addresses of boatbuilders.

Nielsen-Kellerman Co., 201 E. Tenth St., Marcus Hook, PA 19061. Manufacturers of the Strokecoach and other interesting electronic goodies.

Concept II, Inc., RR 1, Box 1100, Morrisville, VT 05661-9727. Manufacturers of Concept II sculls and ergometer.

Suggestions for Further Reading

Bolger, Philip C. *100 Small Boat Rigs*. Camden, Maine: International Marine Publishing Co., 1984.

Brown, Bruce C. *Stroke!* Camden, Maine: International Marine Publishing Co., 1986. How to get started in sliding-seat rowing.

Cunningham, Gerry, and Margaret Hanson. *Lightweight Camping Equipment*. New York: Charles Scribner's Sons, 1959.

Fairfax, John, and Sylvia Cook. *Oars Across the Pacific*. New York: W.W. Norton & Co., 1973. The story of a transpacific row.

Gardner, John. *Building Classic Small Craft*. Vols. 1 and 2. Camden, Maine: International Marine Publishing Co., 1977 and 1984. Full of information on the design, history, and use of traditional rowing and sailing boats.

——————. *The Dory Book*. Camden, Maine: International Marine Publishing Co., 1978. The definitive work on this classic rowing boat, plus a wealth of information about wooden-boat building.

Hankinson, Ken. *Fiberglass Boatbuilding for Amateurs*. Bellflower, California: Glen-L Marine, 1982.

King, Derek, and Peter Bird. *Small Boat Against the Sea*. Paul Elek, 1976. The story of the first attempt to row around the world.

Kuntzleman, Charles T. *Rowing Machine Workouts*. Chicago: Contemporary Books, Inc., 1985.

Leather, John. *Gaff Rig*. Camden, Maine: International Marine Publishing Co., 1970. (out of print, but available through libraries)

_____. *Sail and Oar*. Camden, Maine: International Marine Publishing Co., 1982. A survey of designs, mostly traditional. (out of print, but available through libraries)

_____. *Spritsails & Lugsails*. London: Granada Publishing, 1970.

Rousmaniere, John. *The Annapolis Book of Seamanship*. New York: Simon & Schuster, 1983. Written for sailors, this very detailed work contains a wealth of vital information. Read the chapters on first aid, anchoring, weather, and navigation, if nothing else.

Steward, Robert M. *Boatbuilding Manual*. 3rd ed. Camden, Maine: International Marine Publishing Co., 1987.

Index

Training Log

A training log can be a great benefit to any oarsman, particularly an endurance rower. A sample is enclosed to get you started. Under "Location/Course" you can enter anything that will remind you of where you rowed, such as "Angel Island, around Alcatraz to port," or "from Spanish Landing to San Diego Yacht Club." Under "Conditions," note weather, tide, chop, or anything else that may affect your rowing. The "Notes" entry constitutes a record of any changes in the boat, how you rowed, whether or not you did drills, how you felt, etc.

Date *11/14/87*

Location/Course *Dana Point, beach to bell buoy*

Conditions *Cold offshore wind at 10-12 knots, 2-foot chop*

Notes *Raised oarlocks 1/8 inch for chop. Did 15 minutes of no-feather drill at the start. Once offshore, rowed with a little less lean forward and layback to improve stability. Should have raised oarlocks another 1/8 inch.*

Distance *7 1/2 miles*

Time *1 hour 20 minutes*